P9-EDY-451

THEY KNEW PAUL BUNYAN

BY E. C. BECK

ILLUSTRATED BY ANITA ENEROTH

ANN ARBOR: THE UNIVERSITY OF MICHIGAN PRESS

THEY KNEW

PAUL BUNYAN

ACKNOWLEDGMENTS

952659

This is my third book to be published by The University of Michigan Press. The others are **Songs of the Michigan Lumberjacks** (1941) and **Lore of the Lumber Camps** (1948). My helpful wife did most of the typing for this volume.

In the summer of 1955 the University of Michigan gave me a grant to travel, collect, and write, which made it possible for me to visit old-timers in Upper Michigan, Lower Michigan, and Wisconsin and to travel the timber country in Wyoming, Montana, Idaho, Washington, and Oregon. It made possible the earlier completion of this work.

Above all, I am grateful to those lumberjack entertainers with whom I have associated for two decades: the rugged old shanty boys who have gone to their last wanigans, and men like George Hedquist, Leon May, Bill Monigal, and Billie Girard, who are still excellent sources.

E. C. BECK

Mt. Pleasant, Michigan   January 1, 1956

FOREWORD

There is romance in lumber. From Maine to Washington, in cities like Bangor, Saginaw, Muskegon, Eau Claire, Rainy River, and Seattle the rugged lumberjack in his bright red or green mackinaw has left his manly imprint.

In the Northeast and in the Great Lakes region the jacks went into the woods in the fall and didn't come down the river until the spring floods, agilely riding the logs with their calked shoes. They strode into towns like Bangor and Saginaw with a big roll of bills and a big thirst—they rid themselves of both in jig time. During the long winters the choppers, sawyers, teamsters, and swampers sat around the shanties from mess to bedtime and told tall tales, like about the time Paul Bunyan's ox Babe was crossing Herring Lake over the ice and broke through a thin spot. He spilled the whole load of peas he had been toting. The crew would have had no supper if Big Ben the cook hadn't built a fire under the lake and boiled up some pea soup.

There are woodsmen of fame besides Paul Bunyan. One of them is Joe Muffreau—or Joe Murphy if the storyteller happens to be Irish—who made his reputation logging the Mistassini River in Quebec. Fred

Chaperon claims to have received from Joe a letter recounting his meeting with Paul: "I will endeavor to give you an idea of the size of the real Paul Bunyan, something no other man has been able to give the public without resorting to untruths.

"From the soles of his feet to the roots of his hair he split the atmosphere exactly 12 feet 11 inches. His weight, he told me—and I don't doubt his word—was 888 pounds. . . . When he opened his mouth in one of his prodigious yawns, you could have inserted a ten-quart pail."

The shanty boys bragged about narrow escapes and other adventures, sang old and homemade songs, and danced stag dances. Now and then a camp musician was a master on the fiddle or dulcimer. He was sometimes helped in making his music by a pal playing a pair of beef rib bones furnished by the cook or a couple of tablespoons from the kitchen, or maybe an empty beer keg with a deer skin stretched taut over one end.

The Northwest has been the home of an adventurous lot of toppers. They are responsible for numerous good anecdotes. The men who raft the logs in Canada and Pacific America have furnished a fair share of interesting stories. The songs of this section do not differ much from earlier songs sung in lumber camps farther east, probably because the phonograph and then radio interfered with original composition. Folks furnish their own entertainment only when they must.

Every attempt has been made to identify each song or story with the lumberjack or lumberjill who first furnished it. It is not my intention to publish in this volume any tall stories that have been published by some other writer. The generation who originated this folk material is largely gone—it is becoming increasingly difficult to collect folklore of the woods.

Though I have visited pulp wood men from Minnesota to Florida, talked with cypress lumbermen in southern Florida and Louisiana, been at the long leaf pineries in Alabama and western Florida and at the tie camps in Wyoming and Colorado, listened to the tall-fir timbermen in Washington and Oregon, and watched the Canadian drives in Ontario and Quebec, I have found that the concentration of good tales and songs has been in the Great Lakes lumber camps. These shanty boys have furnished much of what is printed between these covers.

CONTENTS

CHAPTER I

TALL TALES
FROM THE
THICK TIMBER

For it happened in that winter
When the snow was deep and blue.
I can bring a thousand lumberjacks
Who'll swear this tale is true.

Whether Briton, Gael, Scandinavian, French-Canadian, or Finn, the lumberjacks were rugged, hard-muscled, and big-hearted. They had their code and it was a chivalrous one. Rough in dress and speech and manners, they gained their livelihood by the hardest kind of manual labor, living, loving, and laughing crudely.

Picturesque names were legion. The following men may not tell stories like Walter Gries of Ishpeming, Burr Sherwood of Crystal Falls, Thomas Beaton of Escanaba, Dr. Buckland of Baraga, or Bill Robinson of Amasa, but, as Ned Buntline taught us, there is something in a name: Rattlesnake Jim, Tanbark Bill, Big Eric, Peerless Grice, Cedar Root Charley, Big Swede, Dynamite Jack, Indian Joe, Paddy the Pig, Blowhard Ike, Chris Crosshaul, Roaring Jim, Billy the Bum, Rollway Jack, Man-eater Cunyan, Good John, Frying-pan Mag, Double-breasted Dave, Blue Jay, Pigfoot, Black Jack, Stub Foot, Old Lightheart, Pump-handle Joe, Stuttering Jim, Rocky Dan, Smart Alec, Ginpole Johnson, Slabwood Johnson, Cordwood Johnson.

The lumberjacks, or shanty boys, who cut the logs and ran them to the mills were a colorful lot. This letter, picked up from one of the many people who helped me collect woods material, illustrates a certain kind of color.

"Nogi P. O.
April 17, '09

Dear Boss: I been write you for one job on drive. Firs, I tole you what I cant do. I got 25 year hole and been follow dis work for las four or five year, I don't mak no brag on myself but you cant find noder man do so much what I cant. All I want is good pavee [peavey] and I do your work. I got big family and need work verry bad. I been roun long tam and find no work. I guarantee my work satisfy me.

Your truly,
Joe Troudeau

S. P.   When you write let me no."

The literature of the lumber camps grew up around the wood stove or on the deacon seat from the time the jacks finished their talkless meal until bedtime, which was about nine o'clock. The deacon seat, in early lumbering of Maine and adjacent timber country, was originally made of one-half of a log, flat side up, running the length of the bunkhouse. The axe and the saw provided that early American creation. The "deacon" was the fellow who was able to read and sing, the cultured gentleman deserving the best seat in the house. As lumbering moved west into Michigan and Wisconsin, the deacon's seat, instead of being made by skilled axemen, was put together with sawn boards hauled from the sawmill. The deacon seat was the stage Saturday night in the shanty for any jack who could sing, play the harmonica, or tell a good story. If a would-be performer turned bashful and refused to do his stuff, the roughnecks could convince him by a blanket-tossing session. These same entertainments were offered week after week and enjoyed by the crew.

Among the best storytellers from beyond the Great

Lakes whom I have known are Hank Peters of Nova Scotia, Perry Greene of Maine, and Charley Trollope of Nebraska. Besides those from whom I heard the stories printed in this chapter, I must mention Peerless Grice of Marion, Bird Williams of Tustin, Ike Trudo of Ishpeming, Bud Goodman of Negaunee, Wyman Buck of Greenville, Blinkey Adams of Tawas City, Bill Amick of Grand Rapids, Dan Carey of Mt. Pleasant, Fred Ottmar of DeWitt, James Stanley of Farwell, C. K. Hansen of Scottville, Abraham Nelson of Ludington, Bill Monigal of Iron Mountain, and Joe Baillairgeon of Fremont.

America loves its tall stories. That fact isn't really surprising when you think that the pioneers who loved such Rabelaisian tales, and their successors who still love them, in just a few decades have made out of the wilderness of this hemisphere the greatest nation on earth. Such people have done the impossible, they have a fondness for impossible stories.

The folks of this nation have several well-known "tall" characters: Old Stormalong, Bowleg Bill, Joe Magarac, Tony Beaver, John Henry, Pecos Bill, Gib Morgan. Other such characters are growing up. In Florida I have heard splendid tales of Big John the Conqueror. In the Ozarks I met a fascinating Ab Yancey. In Nebraska my father introduced me to that Swede from the north woods, Febold Feboldson. Among the oil men I have come to have some acquaintance with Joe Skirl, or Joe Squirrel. In the Wisconsin woods I have heard some rumors of a Whiskey Jack.

Among all these tall characters Paul Bunyan is best known. Bunyan stories more or less obscene and profane were known before the twentieth century. In fact, Paul Bunyan was mentioned in books before 1900. Perry Allen and Bill McBride and Tom Jones, three of my best original sources, all swore they heard Bunyan stories in the 1880's. It is to be supposed that these stories circulated orally for some years before any of them got into print, just as the stories of Baron Munchausen circulated orally for some years before Rudolf Raspe had several of them printed.

Max Gartenberg in the **Journal of American Folklore** (62:416) has made a good case for Paul Bunyan's coming from Bon Jean "as representative of the French peasant mind." As for me, I just cannot form a stable opinion as to where Paul was born. He could have come into the states with the French-Canadians, though I can see no way to prove this. In spite of my contacts with a great many lumberjacks, I cannot say whether he was born in Maine, Michigan, or Minnesota, but he was born before the Northwest became king of the pines. He did migrate to the Pacific timber—whether or not he dragged his pick and formed the Grand Canyon.

Camp cooks are not among the worst storytellers; they will tell tales about things like vinegar pies, daily kegs of molasses cookies, mile-high piles of sourdough pancakes, and triweekly kegs of fried cakes. Tom Beaton of Escanaba tells this one about Jack Reno, an Upper Michigan cook with very little schooling. Jack made some doughnuts and couldn't understand why they weren't so good. He insisted he had used all the right ingredients. When Jack showed the sack from which he had taken the flour for the doughnuts, it turned out that he had used pancake flour. The lumberjacks asked him why he thought he had used doughnut flour. On the sack was printed DO NOT KEEP IN A DAMP PLACE. Jack displayed this to his questioners and said triumphantly, "See, that says doughnut, D-O-N-O-T."

Probably the best-known cook of Upper Michigan was Widow Phelan, of the American Soo. Chefs of the Muskegon drives include Art Harrison, Henry Bellinger, Joe DuChin, Frank LaVigne, Johnny Glea-son, Alec Axford, and the three Gordons. Among the women cooks were Mrs. Frank Flarity, of Nessen City, with Buckley and Douglas; Mrs. Christine Nelson, of Maple City, with Nemeskal; Mrs. Mary Conklin, of Eastport, with Noble and Dexter; Mrs. Russell Wood, of Pellston, with Tindall and Jackson.

Speaking of food, John Barten, foreman for Josiah Littlefield of Farwell, skinned a couple of bull mosquitoes and brewed some excellent soup. Tennessee Miller told almost the same story on Reelfoot Lake, except Miller roasted his mosquitoes for a "scrumptious Sunday dinner."

Leon May, known among the old shanty boys as "the camp cook from Fife Lake," was an excellent entertainer. He must have been popular in the shanties on long winter nights, for Leon could strum a good guitar or mandolin, could play the piano and violin with the best, could sing a hundred songs, was the best square-dance caller in the woods, and did all right with his tall tales.

One evening Leon held forth on Paul Bunyan: "There have been so many so-called tall tales of the Paul Bunyan camps that it seems to me that it is about time that someone straightened out some of the facts about the camp and told those facts as they really are. You see, some of these things are being taught as reading matter, and I wouldn't want the youngsters finding out later that some of those so-called facts wasn't true. So I'm going to tell you some real facts about Paul Bunyan.

"You see, I was born not far from Old Paul's camp on the Tobacco River. Kinda funny how that river got its name. 'Twas just a little crick when Old Paul set up his camp there. Mighty fine cold water. Old Paul figured it would be just right for the cook to use and the boys to drink. Well, sir, that winter the boys sat around the camp an awful lot because of heavy snow, and setting around there, they chawed an awful lot of tobacco. [It was Peerless or Jolly Tar or Niggerwool.] Old Paul always treated his help right, and he issued a pound of plug to each man each morning. Well, sir, setting around the camp, they chawed and spit and spit and chawed, all the time spitting out the window. When it thawed out in the spring, instead of that crick being nice and clear it was brown with tobacco juice. From that time to now it has been called Tobacco River. And do you know that was where they first started catching brown trout in Michigan?

"Well, as I said, I was raised near there, and when Old Paul moved his camp over by Houghton Lake I was pretty lonesome. I made up my mind that as soon as I got growed up I'd go up there to work.

"When I got my growth, I was only five feet and thirteen inches tall. Now, all the men in Paul's camp were eight feet or more, so I was given a job as choreboy. That's how I got to know so much about what went on in camp.

"Now just for instance, there's that yarn about the cook strapping hams on the feet of the choreboys and having them skate around on pancake griddles to grease them. Now, anybody knows that ain't true. You just can't fasten a ham onto a feller's feet like that. Let's get that matter straight once and for all. Them wasn't hams he strapped on their feet. Them was slabs of bacon.

"Well, sir, I worked in camp eighteen months that winter. When I first came to camp, Johnny Inkslinger was clerking there and keeping the time. That was where I saw my first fountain pen. Johnny had so much writing to do and had to work so fast that he hooked up a length of hose onto a barrel of ink and fastened the other end of that hose to his pen. He estimated that he saved 1 hour, 17 minutes, 38 seconds each day by not having to dip his pen into the ink. Old Paul was careful about saving time and doing things the shortest and fastest way. Johnny was a beautiful writer, and he could write pretty fast too. Why, you know, one night after supper and before he went to bed, he wrote the entire Webster's Dictionary and never missed dotting an i or crossing a t; he didn't leave out any commas or periods either. But he used so much ink dotting i's and crossing t's that Old Paul told him to cut both out. Do you know he saved a barrel and a half of ink that winter?

"The first job I did for Paul was to help him build a rain barrel. That must have been the biggest rain barrel that ever was built. It held 989 barrels, 28 gallons, 1 quart, ½ pint, 1 gill, and 3 tablespoons full, lacking 8 drops. I know that's right because I measured it carefully.

"That was the winter of the blue snow, the coldest winter Michigan ever knew. It got down to 73¼ degrees below zero, and every degree was a foot long. It was so cold that it took me 2 days and 9 minutes to light a match on a steam grindstone. It got so cold that it froze the flames in the lamps, and we couldn't blow them out. So we just broke off the flames and threw them out of the windows. Most of them we threw out. But when we ran out of pepper, the cook ground some of them up for seasoning. When spring came, those flames thawed out and started a fire in the woods. That fire ran clean to St. Mary's River and burned it in two. Of course, this held up navigation and made the water back up in Lake Superior so that the folks up at Duluth wrote Old Paul and asked him what he was going to do about it. So the next morning Old Paul took one of the wagon boxes off a wagon and a shovel and went up there and put that wagon box in where the river was burned in two. That was the first ship canal at the Soo. It was quite a job, and Old Paul was 18 minutes late for dinner.

"Now, when it began to thaw in the spring, it began to rain, and it rained so hard and so fast that the water running off the roof of the shanty ran into that rain barrel faster than it could run out. You know, that water piled right up above the top of the barrel until it was 3 feet 11 inches above the top. Why, it rained so hard that Houghton Lake began to slop over the sides. So Paul took Babe the blue ox and plowed a furrow from the lake down to Lake Michigan. He didn't dare wait until daylight because it was raining so hard. Having to plow the furrow at night in the black darkness, he couldn't see so good, and that is why the Muskegon River is so crooked.

"As soon as spring came, Old Paul gave me a job wheeling chips. You see, when he cut a log in two he chopped so fast that the chips would pile up in his way, so that he couldn't see where he was chopping. The job I had was to use a wheelbarrow to wheel away the chips when he went out to chop logs. When I went back into camp, I had to hitch up a team of ponies that he had in the barn and drive the salt-and-pepper wagon. That cook shanty was so big, and the crew was so big that a lot of time was wasted passing salt and pepper shakers; so the blacksmith rigged up a wagon and the cook would load it with salt and pepper, and I drove that wagon up and down the length of the table so the boys could help themselves. I did not have it so easy on Sundays either because on Sundays we had prunes for breakfast. I was busy most of the day hauling out prune pits.

"Now, there's been a lot of talk about Babe the blue ox. Babe wasn't naturally blue. He was as white as any ox until the winter of the blue snow. Old Paul was over in Vermont the morning the snow started to fall; he noticed that it was rather odd for color, so he rode Babe home as fast as he could. They got home a little after eleven. I can't tell the exact time, but it was just before dinner. But Babe had been out in that blue snow, and he never changed color after that. He was always blue thereafter.

"Paul kept Babe around for several years, but he didn't do so good. He seemed kinda lifeless and pindeling, and finally Paul decided that he was lonesome. So Paul rode him down to Texas one morning to see if he could find him a cow to keep Babe company. He kinda thought too that it would help with the milk bill. Now, Babe was the best trained riding ox I ever saw. Just yell "Whoa," and he'd stop dead still anywhere. Well, as Paul was riding him over the mountains, he came to a deep chasm, better than a hundred feet deep. They were going so fast that they couldn't stop. Over the chasm they went. Paul kept his head and remembered how well Babe had been trained, and he yelled "Whoa!" Babe stopped just 9 feet 7 inches from the bottom, and Paul got off without even a scratch.

"Well, Paul found a cow down in Texas, one that just suited him. Paul didn't want a cow as big as Babe for fear Babe would get an inferiority complex. You see Babe weighed 8,246 pounds. He was 11 feet tall, and was two axe-handles and a thumb between the eyes. His horns had a spread of 16 feet 4 inches. Babe bellowed only once in his life. That time it jarred the earth so hard that that volcano over in Italy broke loose, and Paul had to put a stop to that.

"The pine that we cut around Houghton Lake was some of the finest I ever saw. The trees stood just ten feet apart. The first winter Paul had no teams in the woods; he used Babe only. Now, I'll bet you're saying that somebody is falsifying, that if Babe's horns spread 18 feet, how could he be used when the trees was only ten feet apart. Well, sir, that just goes to show you don't know nothing about Michigan logging. That was easy. Paul had the blacksmith make some hinges for Babe's horns. When he worked in the woods, we just folded his horns back and got along just dandy. The only time we had any trouble was that cold spell I was talking about. You see, we folded them horns down when we went out that morning, and it turned cold so quick that we did not have time to straighten them out before they froze. Babe went around for seven weeks before it got warm enough to straighten them out.

"That Babe was sure a great ox to pull. One day Old Paul was hauling logs with him on good sledding ice. Babe was pulling for all he was worth. Paul didn't think and laid his buckskin mittens on that load of logs. Babe stopped. He was stuck. Paul took the mittens off the load and Babe pulled it along like nothing. That just goes to show you how Babe could measure his strength. Paul's mittens were kind of heavy.

"Well, the winter after Paul got the cow we ran out of hay, so we had to feed Babe and his mate on browse. They seemed to do all right on it. But after a little while the milk got so we couldn't use it, it tasted so strong of birch and balsam. Old Paul then ordered a couple of carloads of pint bottles. We bottled that milk and sold it at a dollar a bottle for cough medicine. Funny thing though, when the cow had a calf that spring, its horns were wooden. From that time all her calves had wooden horns, balsam horns one year and birch horns the next.

"That winter we nearly ran out of food. Guess we would of too if it hadn't been for that boiling spring just behind the cook shanty. The teamster that drove the tote team went out after a load of peas. Coming into camp, he tipped over right by the boiling spring, and all the peas went into the water kersplash. When the cook seen what was happening, he ran out with half a hog and a couple of 100-pound boxes of salt pork; he threw them into the spring along with salt and pepper. We had hot pea soup any time of day or night for the rest of the winter.

"In fact, we got kinda tired of pea soup. So Paul thought he would try to rustle up a little fresh meat. Now, Paul was not a bad hunter. Lots of folks don't know that, but it is the truth. I remember one story that is pretty good evidence that Paul could hunt: One summer Paul raised a flock of chickens so that we could have a chicken dinner one Sunday each month. Paul discovered that an old fox from over by Roscommon was stealing his chickens. He hid in a clump of brush and waited for that fox to come out of his den. After a time the fox came out and began playing around. He would keep getting farther and farther from the den until Paul figgered he had gone the limit. Old Paul figgered he'd shoot the fox, but if he missed the tricky old thief, he'd run to the den and head him off. He shot. Well, sir, at the sound of the gun, Mr. Fox headed for the den and so did Paul. The fox got there first with Paul hot behind. As the fox dodged into the den, Paul grabbed him by the tail. Just as he grabbed the tail, that charge of shot struck Old Paul right in the seat of his britches. Paul sure could run. He got the fox too.

"Well, as I was saying, Paul went out one morning with his double-barreled rifle to see what he could find in the way of fresh meat. Paul had to go pretty careful with his shooting, for he had only two loads. Well, over by Roscommon he saw a fawn. Now, a fawn is mighty good eating, and this one was a dandy. It weighed a little over 500 pounds. Paul shot it. The bullet went clean through that fawn and hit a basswood tree. Paul saw something running out of the bullet hole, so he went over to investigate. I'll be dadgummed if it wasn't honey. He had hit a bee tree. After he had dressed the fawn, he walked up to Grayling where he saw a bear. Paul reckoned that a bear was as much meat as he could get for that second shot, so he pulled the trigger. Maybe you won't believe me, but that bullet went clean through the bear and split a limb on a nearby tree. Well, sir, there was seven wild pigeons setting on that limb. When the limb split, their feet dropped into the crack; and when that crack closed, they were caught.

"Old Paul went back to camp, got an axe and two 60-gallon barrels, and went back to where he had shot the fawn. He put the barrels under the hole in the tree so the honey would run into them. Then he went on to where he had shot the bear and climbed up to the limb where the pigeons were fast. Old Paul chopped off that limb, and that was one of the few mistakes Old Paul ever made: he cut off the limb he was setting on.

"When he done that, he fell kersplash into the crick below. Old Paul wore a pair of bib overalls, and when he climbed out of the crick, nine big trout got caught in those overalls. They were so heavy that the weight busted a button off the overalls; that button flew and hit a rabbit square in the eye.

"Well, sir, Old Paul just strung those trout, those pigeons, and that rabbit on his ramrod, slung the bear and deer over his shoulder, tucked the barrel of honey under each arm, and hurried back to camp. Maybe you think that was quite a load, but that ain't nothing to what he could do.

"Once he swum the Manistee River with a ton of loose hay on his back and carried eight quarts of loose blackberries in his hands. Those were some berries too. I never saw such large and juicy berries. We had to squeeze the juice out before we could make pies. We tried to make some once't without squeezing the juice out, and those pies run over in the oven when they were baking. When we opened the oven doors, the pies just floated right out onto the kitchen floor. We never tried that again.

"When winter broke up, the wild ducks began to come back north. Since meat was short again, Paul went out to get a mess of ducks. Paul knew where the ducks fed, and he started for the feeding grounds. On his way there he saw a flock of wild geese flying over, and he took a shot at them. They were so high up in the air that he couldn't tell whether he hit any of them or not. When he got to the feeding grounds, he saw about fifty ducks feeding in a ditch. They were standing on the bank with their heads down in the ditch water. Paul figgered that if he could get them to raise their heads all at the same time, he could shoot the heads off all of them with one shot. He whistled. Up came the heads of all them ducks; but just as Paul pulled the trigger, a mosquito lit on his nose and spoiled his aim. Instead of shooting the heads off the ducks, he shot the bills off all fifty of them.

"Paul never done much hunting after that. Soon afterwards he went out to hunt and his gun blew up. So he took the gun barrels and used them for smoke-stacks on his shingle mill. The old stacks were too short. That was a big mill and needed big stacks. You know, if they lighted a fire under the boilers on Monday morning, it was half past two on Wednesday morning before the smoke began to come out of the stacks. When the air was heavy, two men were stationed at the top of the stacks to shovel the smoke away.

"As quick as the ice went out in the spring, Paul began to get ready for the drive. He had to build some dams in the stream to raise the water high enough to float his logs. But by spring he was ready for the drive. He had been training a bunch of beaver all winter; as soon as the ice went out he set those beaver to work. Just as soon as they finished one dam, he'd start them on another. It wasn't long before the dams was built.

"We started out one morning and drove for two days, never seeing a sign of anyone until long after sundown of the second day, when we passed a mighty big camp. We didn't stop. We kept right on going for a couple more days when we passed another big camp. But the logs were running good and fast, so we didn't stop there either. In about two more days we came to another camp. The funny thing was that these three camps looked a lot alike. Do you know that when we stopped at this third camp, it was our own camp? We had passed that camp three times. You see, we were on Round River. Round River has no beginning or end, it just runs in a circle. Well, Old Paul was in a hurry to get them logs to Muskegon; so he went out the next morning with his shovel and dug a ditch from there over to where he had plowed the furrow from Houghton Lake to Muskegon.

"As soon as the drive was over, I came back home. Old Paul moved his camps to Minnesota that summer, and it was too far for me to walk, so I stayed around here ever since.

"Now these are some facts about Paul Bunyan's camp. I could tell you some real whoppers about Old Paul, but you must remember that I am trying to sort out the truths."

Mrs. William Bryan of Lake Ann recalled that Big Ben, Paul Bunyan's cook, was quite a character. He couldn't be "stumped." He was hired to feed the big crew and see that they were well filled; he always did. Everyone knows it was Ben who invented split pea soup. Once he ran shy of soup for supper, so he split the peas and doubled the amount of soup.

Jack Kelly of Empire did nothing one winter but fill Paul's pipe. "It took a ton of Peerless to a filling. Niggerwool was a little stronger and Paul used less of it. He preferred Peerless." It was Jack, I believe, who tried unsuccessfully to grow plug tobacco in the plug.

"Paul had his blue ox on the Betsie River one season," Jack reminisced. "When Babe—that's the blue ox, you know—had to leave Benzie County, he cried so hard that he made Crystal Lake, Platte Lake, Herring Lake, and many smaller lakes."

There are a lot of stories about the woods that don't concern Paul Bunyan. They are nonetheless tall: F. A. Lamoreaux of Grand Rapids said that Tom Canard, who worked for C. C. Comstock of Grand Rapids, had a deer try to leap over his load of logs. The deer realized he could not make it, paused in midair, turned and went back.

While hunting deer, lumberjack Jim Royce of Blanchard ran out of balls, so he shot his ramrod through the deer. When Jim quit lumbering and went to farming, he made a reputation for his clear cider; he filtered it through a two-inch plank.

Jim Vahey of Leaton like many other jacks tilled the soil in the summer and cut logs in the winter. Jim was shocking wheat one hot summer day when a deer glided into the field. It seemed tame, so Jim thought he might be able to catch it. Jim ran and ran after that deer. "Jist as I was going to grab the beast," said Jim, "I slipped on the ice. You want to remember I chased that deer a long ways."

Glen D. Meek, who signs his name "Jack from back near Cadillac," though he now lives in Vancouver, Washington, spent his youthful days in the pines of Wexford and Missaukee counties. Meek insists that a Douglas fir will shoot up a whip twice as fast as a white pine. "That is why," said Meek, "that a shingle nail driven in a fir tree was pulled out three years later as a huge bridge spike."

The Great Lakes could almost match such growth, however. The inevitable John Johnson of Minnesota stuck his gimlet in a lightning crack of a pine tree and forgot it. Some years later when the tree was harvested that gimlet had grown into a post auger nine inches in diameter.

Dr. Wilkie M. Drake of Breckenridge tells a story or two about Ebbin Burgin. He can recall the time Ebbin drove his ox team to Ithaca one spring when the roads were so soft the oxen sank from sight and Ebbin kept them going by whipping and guiding the bubbles. Ebbin was in Ithaca when the Tub Factory exploded; he was blown so high that he saw his wife thirty miles away picking up chips.

Irish McEwen of Moorestown is authority for the story of Jim Hunt. Jim got too drunk to find his way home from the Dead Stream but not too drunk to climb a tree for the night. The next morning when Jim was located, he was frozen so stiff that the limb around which he had thrown his arm had to be sawed off before he would fall to the ground. He was tossed in the sleigh like a log and was hauled home and dumped in the water tank. In about thirty minutes his eyes fluttered, and after another thirty minutes he crawled out of the tank.

Tales from the lumber country do not lack humor: Pat Egan of Nessen City had had hash on Friday and the priest found out. The priest suggested that Pat pay for his sin by gathering a load of lumber. Pat came in hauling a load of sawdust.

"This isn't wood, Pat," the priest told him.

Pat answered, "If hash is meat, Father, this is wood."

At Burke's boarding house in Nahma, when Burke's was feeding lumberjacks for the Bay De Noc Lumber Company, I picked up this French-Canadian story: Pierre and Jacques seemed paragons of brotherly devotion. The two were usually together. But once, while Pierre was up-river, the agile Jacques slipped and was crushed by the logs. When the delegation broke the sad news to Pierre, he dropped his canthook and sputtered in impassioned French. Then he began feeling his pockets.

"Calm down," the jacks urged.

"What you mean, calm down," screamed Pierre. "Dis sohn of beech, my brother, he had my bes' pipe."

Some veterans of the woods have a repertory of tales that would fill a volume. Among these are Old Man Brockett of Greenville. Old Man Brockett was a swamper, and since the teamsters got up about half past four, the swampers who helped the teamsters could not stay in bed much later. The teamsters were the men who drove the horses and mules, whether for the supply wagon or for hauling logs or skidding. The teamsters were always the first men in camp to get up. They had to feed, clean, and harness their horses. And every day was precious because the logs had to be moved before the break-up of the ice roads along which the logs were hauled to the rivers. Usually, the man owned his own team and the company hired both him and his horses; hence, the name teamster. After a tree was felled, it was the job of the swamper to cut off the branches so the sawyers could cut the trunk into suitable log lengths. He also had to clear away all the bushes and trees that might hinder the skidding of a log on its way to a suitable place for loading onto a sleigh. The teamsters skidded the logs by attaching to the log what looked very much like tongs used to pick up blocks of ice (only of course much larger). The team of horses or oxen then drew it to a skidway or rollway where it was loaded on the sleigh for hauling to the river.

One story that Old Man Brockett tells goes like this: One early morning as he stepped out of his shanty, he saw before him in the fresh snow a huge bear. Noiselessly he backed into the shanty, took a gun off the wall, slipped out of the door again, took good aim and "let him have it."

The bear hardly moved. It seemed to be standing up and grinning at him.

Brockett slipped back into the shanty, reloaded the gun, came out, took careful aim, and fired. The results were the same. Four more times he loaded and fired. Still the bear was grinning at him.

He thought he had better investigate. So he investigated. And do you know what he found? He had a greyback on his eyelash. The greyback is the lumberjack louse. The large bunkhouse of the past had bunks filled with swamp grass or hay or straw. Two lumberjacks to the bunk, their mackinaws or pants were pillows, no mattress, three thick warm blankets.

Most lumberjacks were clean, and on Sunday they boiled their clothing in the large iron kettles located outside, using lots of strong yellow laundry soap. Some lumberjacks were drifters or floaters, "roamin' here, roamin' there, and I don't care," usually dirty and unkempt, ideal for the louse family. When this drifter hit the bunkhouse, his cursed pests started to migrate into clean bunks for new blood. When the old camp broke up in the spring, the drifters and their pests had loused up the bunks and the smelly blankets. Even some of the faithful dobbins were lousy and required washing. Peerless tobacco steeped in boiling water, powerful King Nicotine, knocked out the greyback.

Then there was the day when Brockett was hunting with his muzzle-loader. Seeing nine partridges sitting side by side on a log, he took the shot out of the muzzle and put the ramrod in. Then he shot those partridges, all nine of them, through their heads, stringing them all on the ramrod.

One day while watching the Flat River near his home, he noticed an island he had never seen before. It was a smooth rounded island without grass or trees. So he got into his canoe and paddled out to the island. Its smooth, greenish-gray surface interested him, and he lingered until the afternoon sun put him to sleep. When he awoke about sundown, he found himself in Gowen on the back of a snapping turtle.

In central Michigan, especially in Isabella and Clare counties, Jim Vahey's name is legend. He was a raw-boned, broad-shouldered man, over six feet tall, with sandy hair and beard. He always had one pants leg rolled higher than the other. He had a slight limp. He explained the limp this way: "When the Carey boys and me was lumbering for Fields up in Roscommon County, I was standing at the bottom of a rollway that was a 200-foot precipice. Standing on solid rock with a canthook in hand, I caught logs as they came down. Over the ledge came a maple log of about five hundred feet. I nailed that log, and it drove me into solid rock clean up to my knees. If you'll jist take notice, you'll see I'm still lame from it."

Jim farmed during the summers. When he brought his wheat to market, he hitched a small horse and a large one to his wagon. On main street he was stopped by a wiseacre citizen, who called out, "Jim, one of your horses is way ahead of the other."

Jim called "Whoa" and crawled off the wagon seat. He came around in front of the horses, took a long look, and drawled, "Hell, that ain't bad. The big one is only three feet ahead of the little one, and we been going six miles. Three feet in six miles, that ain't much of a gain."

Vahey insisted that his land was so rich that he couldn't grow pumpkins. The earth was so fertile that the vines grew fast enough to wear out the pumpkins as they were dragged along. He did grow a few one season by putting the blooms in little wagons and having the pumpkins develop on wheels. His beets grew so that they crowded the Pere Marquette railroad tracks over onto the next farm. Several of the big ones had to be pulled with winches, and they left holes in the ground that filled with water and became sizable lakes.

A tale often told in Isabella County involves Jim Vahey and the beloved Father O'Connor. Jim met Father downtown, and after an exchange of greetings Father asked Jim, "Do you know where I can buy a good cow?"

"What kind of a cow do you want, Father?"

"A Jersey cow, I believe, Jim. One that will give good rich milk."

"I've got just the cow for you."

"How much milk does she give?" queried the kindly Father.

"To tell you the truth, Father, I don't know. You see, when we milk her, we put the wash-tub under her; my wife gets on one side and I get on the other and we milk till the tub is full. Then we give the cow a push and tell her to get along."

Frequently Jack Fathey, who spent his last years in the Midland area, told his best stories when arguing with Alec Thorpe. Alec liked to tell about his success in crossing hoot-owls with other animals. He first crossed hoot-owls with woodpeckers to produce the hoot-pecker, which never slept and which later was sent to the Northwest to fight the spruce beetle around the clock. He also tried a cross between hoot-owls and nanny goats; that is how the hoot-nanny came into being. He went almost too far when a Scotchman eloped with one of his fairest owls; the firstborn was the original hoot-man. Jack was once a choreboy for Bradley and Turner in a lumber camp on the Tittabawassee River. One of his tasks was to bring the cows across the river each evening. The ingenious choreboy tied fish-hooks to the cows' tails and baited the hooks. Almost every night when the cows waded out on the camp side of the river, fish would be hanging to their tails. Then Jack would run the cows through the blackberry bushes to scale the fish. The cook finished cleaning the catch, and the jacks had fresh fish for supper.

Jack said he built a sawmill for Paul Bunyan over on the Little Onion River. The boiler was built of hardwood with rock elm flues. The smokestack was so high that it took the "hull of three months" for the smoke to come out of the top. "This wasn't no small shakes of a mill," Jack contended. "It took three railroads to haul off the cut for a day. The sawdust got so that every night when we come out of the mill there'd be a pile a hundred feet high covering about 180 acres. Paul seen that we had to do something about that; so he sent to Chicago for a carload of green goggles. When they come, Paul had his hull flock of cows sent up to camp. He fitted a pair of them goggles on each of them cows. It worked, all right. The danged cows et the hull pile of sawdust—they thought it was grass. But the milk tasted like that pine tar cough medicine."

"One year," Jack mused, "Paul had me set out about 800 acres of lead pencil plants. It was a good spring, and purty soon them lead pencil plants got to six inches high and started to rubber.

"About that time them plants bloomed into the

purtiest red, white, and blue blossoms you ever seen. What kind of fruit them blossoms would have produced, no one ever knew, for the blackbirds come in thousands to pick off them flowers. Paul had a couple of old howitzers he'd got somewheres. He loaded them with bird shot with just enough powder to blow off the feathers without killing the birds. He hired boys to pick up the feathers, and he started a feather-bed factory in Midland. That was before Mr. Dow come to town. The naked birds flew back south where it was warmer, but they always come back to gather them blossoms each spring. That is what kept the factory going. That was before Mr. Dow found them chemical wells, you must remember."

It was Jack who named Michigan's Tobacco River. He had noticed that Ontario raised tobacco, and he could not understand why tobacco couldn't be raised in Michigan. A lumbercamp ran on plug tobacco and snuff, so there should be profit in this crop.

He sent down to Kentucky and had tobacco plants sent to him. Down by the river he set out about eighty acres of these plants. As the plants grew into good healthy stalks, Jack was thinking that this tobacco growing was strictly an experiment, and he wondered if he could run the risk of a no-crop year. So, to play safe, he planted across the rail fence from his tobacco field about seventy acres of cabbage, because cabbage was almost a certain crop and sold well to the "Saginaw Irish."

"Both crops done fine," said Jack. "The tobacco had nice wide furry leaves. The cabbage heads grew to four, five, six pounds. It looked like I'd hit the jackpot when them danged grasshoppers moved in. You know, they et up every stalk of that tobacco. Not satisfied with that, them danged hoppers set on the rail fence and chawed that tobacco and spit the tobacco juice all over them cabbages. I thought I was ruined when a idea hit me. I pulled them cabbages and ground them up; they made the best grade of Copenhagen that Michigan ever had."

The truth of the tale is proved by the fact that the river on whose banks the tobacco was grown has been known ever since as the Tobacco River.

It is T. J. Carson of Saginaw who knows the geology of Hudson Bay. "Paul, the one I knew, had lived in Siberia. One day during a violent windstorm he climbed a tree just for the hell of it. After he got to the top it started to blow eighteen hurricanes. A few minutes later the tree and Paul went sailing off into space.

"After traveling for days in the air, Paul began to drop. When he struck the earth he skidded, and he made a hole over 900 miles long and many miles wide. Paul was exhausted and fell asleep before investigating his surroundings. While he slept he had a terrible nightmare, which caused him to sweat so much that the hole filled with water. Years afterwards Henry Hudson found this hole and named it Hudson Bay after himself."

Carl Lathrop of Pleasant Valley had heard that Paul had been in Siberia. George Pixley of Harrison claimed that Paul captured the blue ox in Siberia; no one else seems to agree with them except T. J. Carson. T. J., like many Saginaw men, was familiar with the Northwest. He knew Paul Bunyan in the Pacific forests. In fact, he has seen Paul top his own trees in Oregon and thus save the high wages paid "high climbers."

One day Paul stopped on the Columbia River, where he found some really big fish. In fact, they were so big that Paul could eat only half a fish per meal. Paul loved these fish and consequently lumbered along the Columbia for thirty years. Then he noticed that the fish were getting smaller. Finally, it took 3,224 fish for a meal, and they were almost red. The river itself was growing brownish. That is why Paul left the Columbia. Ten years afterwards the Indians found a quid of Paul's tobacco obstructing the headwaters. It took twelve tribes four years to move it. The river cleared up in a few months, but the fish remained small and red. The Indians called them salmon, which in Shoshone is "tobacco fish."

It seems that Bunyan-type tales are not unknown to the Indians. Blue Cloud of the Au Sable Ottawas had a hunting cat. There were many hunting dogs in the community, but Blue Cloud had the only hunting cat. The cat got so good that the master never had to hunt for his meat. One morning the cat would have a rabbit at the doorstep, the next morning he would have a partridge.

Then one morning the cat didn't show up. For several mornings the cat didn't appear, and Blue Cloud had to start hunting again. In about two weeks the cat came back with all its ribs showing and a front leg gone. It had been caught in a trap and had taken two weeks to break out, leaving that leg in the process.

Blue Cloud fed the cat generously, and the cat regained its strength. He still limped of course. So the Ottawa thought he would remedy the cripple; he

whittled out a peg leg for the cat. With that peg leg the cat got around almost as good as ever. Soon he was bringing rabbits to the door again.

"I wonder how that cat manages to catch a rabbit," Blue Cloud said to his wife.

"Why don't you trail him and find out?" suggested his wife.

So one morning Blue Cloud set out to watch his hunter cat. The cat wandered off around a hill and began circling a hollow stump. "There is a rabbit in that stump," thought Blue Cloud.

Sure enough, pretty soon a rabbit dashed out of the stump, the cat pounced on him and beat him to death with that peg leg.

Not to be outdone, Big Tooth told of his cat. He never had liked cats very well, and this particular cat had all the bad habits. One day when the cat robbed a bird's nest, justice came rapidly and finally. Big Tooth chopped off the cat's head.

"Though I knew that cats have nine lives, I never expected this one to prove the saying. But you know, next morning when I stepped outside there was that darned cat sitting on the step holding its head in its mouth."

Alfred Anderson of Monitor Township in Bay County recounted some tales about life in the woods: "In our camp the lumberjacks would take off their shirts and put them in a big iron kettle of boiling water. They would stir and stir with a short pikepole. After a while the lice would come to the top and float around. The jacks would skim them off with a tin pail and throw them away for the wolves to pick. Nobody believes me, but that is as true as I'm here.

"We had some drinking jacks in camp," he continued. "One of them was coming back to camp with a bottle of whiskey in his top pocket. He stopped at the spring to get a drink. While he was drinking, the cork came out of his bottle and all the whiskey ran into the spring. He lay there a day and a half drinking until he recovered all that whiskey. He was so drunk that he had to swallow twelve bottles of Hinkley's Bone Liniment to sober up. Nobody believes me, but that is as true as I'm here."

Though the South may be more familiar with John Henry and Tony Beaver, it has met Paul Bunyan. In the woods operated by St. Regis Paper of West Florida and around the mills of Brewton, Alabama, good stories are abundant.

J. D. C. Williams of Magnolia Springs, Alabama, said that Paul Bunyan had to patch up a bad job on the Pacific coast. Paul realized the size of his job and came all the way to the Gulf of Mexico to get materials. He pulled great tracts of trees out of Alabama and plastered up the California coast. Water rushed into the Alabama holes and formed the very useful Mobile Bay.

It was M. L. Smith, I believe, who heard that Paul had raised some gargantuan watermelons in West Florida. They were so large that when ready for market the melons were loaded on flat cars, two to the car. As the train was going around a river bend, one melon rolled off, burst when it hit the railway grade, and the pieces tumbled into the river, sinking a fishing boat. The fisherman climbed up on one of the black seeds and floated to shore. Several of these melons were used for temporary housing. You see, when they reached their destination in Pensacola, New Orleans, and St. Louis, some of them were cut in half and sold as half melons. The buyers dug out the red delicacy and then turned the rounded side up. In this shell, doors and windows were cut; the result was the first quonset-type house in America.

Old Perry Allen of Shepherd was a clever teller of tall tales as well as a master entertainer with song and dance. One year he won the liar's contest at the Cherry Festival in Traverse City without knowing that he was entered. One time a Washington reporter was interviewing the old lumberjack, and she asked her final question: "And now, Mr. Allen, what about politics?"

"What kind of ticks?" asked the grizzled woodsman.

"Politics," she repeated.

"Well, now, ma'am," puzzled Perry, "I can tell you about bed ticks and cow ticks and wood ticks, but I never heard nothing about polly ticks. I don't think we had 'em."

Old Perry liked to tell the story of how Michigan got its Thumb. As I recall the tale, which I must have heard a hundred times, he told it this way: "One winter that I worked for Hannah and Lay on the Boardman River, Paul Bunyan was our foreman. That spring Mr. Hannah called Paul to the office and said to him: 'Paul, we've run out of timber hereabouts. This Arbutus crew is a good crew, but we have no logs. I hear there is good white pine over on the Huron slope. If you could locate some good tracts of pine, I could give the men some work and make myself some profits at the same time. Pick you out a man, Paul; go over to the Huron shore, and lay me out some lots of good white pine.'

"Paul picked me to go with him. We made a great team, big Him and little Me. We had been timber-looking for a week when we ran out of grub. One afternoon about three o'clock as we were sloshing through the swamp, Paul stopped short and roared 'Perry, we need some fresh meat. Let's go fishing and catch a sturgeon.'

" 'Good idea,' I answered, 'but what will we use for tackle?'

" 'Look up in that treetop,' said Paul. 'See that cable? That's what made me think of it.'

"I looked up in that tree, and sure enough there was a long length of steel cable about an inch in diameter. Don't ask me how it got there. It was there is all I know.

" 'We'll use that for a line,' said Paul.

" 'What about a hook?' I asked.

" 'Remember that swamp-hook we saw back there about a mile?' questioned Paul. 'Go get that while I pull this cable out of the tree.'

"As I started back, Paul yelled, 'And we need bait. Get one of them pigs back there.'

"I waded back through the swamp till I found the hook. I picked it up and brought it back to where the pigs were. You know them shoats were pretty good-sized, about three-months old pigs. I was mighty careful about catching one of them. They must belong to somebody, and I didn't want them to squeal on me. Well, I got one after a time. I slipped the bait under my arm and carried the hook. When I got back to Paul, he had the line down all right. He reached over, took the hook, and gave the line a half-hitch. Then I handed him the bait.

" 'Wait a minute,' said Paul. 'We can't fish from shore. It's too marshy. We'll have to build a raft. Just hold that pig a little while.'

"You know, Paul built a raft in a split second, then reached over for the pig, and carefully strung him on the hook. We crawled onto the raft, threw the hook out into the lake, and waited. We waited and waited and waited. Just about dark we had a helluva strike. The fish got hooked. He took right off for the Canadian shore. We stuck our heels in the raft and held on. All night we speeded around the lake. I saw Detroit three times that night. Come morning, and the fish went to the bottom. It was either tired or it sulked. We looked around and saw that we were not far from shore.

" 'I'm powerful sleepy,' yawned Paul.

" 'I could use a little shut-eye myself,' I replied.

" 'You know, Perry,' said Paul, 'if I could get to the shore and tie up this fish, we could get some sleep. But we can't risk losing this fish now after what we've been through. You stay on the raft just in case the fish starts to move before I reach shore.'

"Do you know, Paul jumped off into Lake Huron. It was deep there. The water came up to his mackinaw. I was left with that fish. My knees played Annie Rooney. But Paul got to shore all right and tied the line to a big elm tree. I hand-over-handed myself to the shore, and we dropped down and had a snooze.

"But, you know, we'd plumb forgot about them Huron Indians. They were around, and they picked where we slept to have a war dance. I woke up with goose pinkles on goose pinkles. But Paul wasn't scared, not of the Indians.

"Paul looked over to me and whispered, 'Perry, they're going to scare that fish.'

"Sure enough, the next war-whoop and the line began to vibrate. Another war-whoop and that fish started right out for the Canadian shore. But the line held and the tree held. That fish pulled that tree and the earth with it right out into the lake. That is how we happen to have a Thumb on Michigan."

Upper Peninsula storytellers include Matt Surrell of Newberry. This tale, collected from Matt in the Tahquamenon country, was printed in **Lore of the Lumber Camps** and is worth republishing:

"Boys, did I ever tell you about the time I drove the Naubinway over to Paul Bunyan's camp on Big Manistique? Boys, I want to tell you there's some thoroughbred mosquitoes over in that swamp even now, but the modern ones are nothing like their ancestors.

"Well, just as I was shoving into Paul's camp that day I heard some terrible droning noises like one of these B-24's. Even Paul, powerful as he was, seemed excited and yelled to me to hurry into his office. So I knew everything wasn't flapjacks and sausage.

"Then Paul told me that some of the big mosquitoes had got loose. He had trapped them five or seven years ago, because they were bothering his cattle. Paul told me that two medium-sized mosquitoes had tried to kill his prize heifer. They had the critter down and were trying to drag her off when along came a really big mosquito. The big one zoomed down, killed the other two, picked up the heifer, and flew away. So Paul decided then and there to put on a campaign against them mosquitoes. He and his men trapped several of them in live traps; the rest got scared and flew away.

"But this particular day, when I come to visit Paul, some of the mosquitoes had broken loose. We barred the doors when he heard the zooming and droning. They began landing on the roof. I shook like an alder leaf, but Paul wasn't scared. Overhead I heard an awful cracking and looked to see swordlike weapons sticking through the roof. Paul said they were mosquito stingers. So he grabbed his sledge and clinched those stingers like a carpenter clinches a nail. Next day he put twelve of his best lumberjacks to executing mosquitoes on that roof. He said he was through showing kindness to mosquitoes. It didn't pay. They'd stab you in the back."

Famous woodsmen besides Paul Bunyan include such legendary figures as Tony Beaver and Febold Feboldson and such actual loggers as Jigger Jones of Maine and Silver Jack of Michigan. Also there is Joe Murphy or Joe Muffreau. This is the entire letter that was supposedly received from Joe Muffreau by Fred Chaperon.

"It was in the early part of the year 1860 that I first met the very lovable but much maligned and lied-about character known to everyone as Paul Bunyan.

"I was chief cook for old Charlie Backus of the Backus Lumber Company doing business on the Au Sable River. The camp was a big one, and the crew was equally big, consisting of 180 big men. When I say big men I mean just that: big men. Not a man of that memorable crew was under 7 feet in height, and none weighed less than 350 pounds.

"To get back to my friend Paul Bunyan. It was in the month of February, 1860. The snow was twenty feet deep on the level. It was, undoubtedly, the worst winter known in the annals of history. I had just finished peeling 180 bushels of potatoes, a chore which had taken me over an hour. I was at that time the fastest undresser of spuds in the north woods.

"I can hear you ask, 'Why 180 bushels of potatoes?' Now, I answered that question before you asked it. Didn't I say we had 180 men? Each man's allowance of potatoes was a bushel a day.

"As I finished the chore I glanced through the window, and the sight which met my eyes made me gasp.

Accustomed as I was to seeing big men, I was totally unprepared for the sight which I saw. What first appeared to be two of our pine trees began moving towards the cook camp door. Hastily grasping the long knife which I had been using to peel the spuds in one hand and a huge cleaver in the other, I opened the door and stepped out to meet the giant. Slowly my eyes began to travel upward to the man's head. Never had I seen such a sight. In my amazement I dropped the knife and cleaver. I was positive I was dreaming until I heard a rumbling sound and realized that the man was speaking.

"I am not a small man myself, being 6 feet 14 inches and tipping the scale at 333 pounds. But this man . . . well . . . what's the use of trying to explain to you tyros of the woods? You wouldn't believe me anyhow. Still, at the risk of being called a prevaricator, I will endeavor to give you an idea of the size of the real Paul Bunyan, something no other man has been able to give the public without resorting to untruths.

"He split the atmosphere exactly 12 feet 11 inches. The rest of his body was built in proportion. Around his hips he measured 12 feet 9 inches; waist, 9 feet 11 inches; shoulders, 14 feet 10 inches; thighs, 6 feet

6 inches; calf, 4 feet 7 inches; and his reach, from here to there, 17 feet 11 inches.

"But what interested me most was his face. He had the most unusual eyes I ever have seen. The distance between his eyes was 17 inches. They were the size of ordinary saucers. His nose resembled a fresh leg of mutton.

"He had, as I afterwards learned, three distinct voices. One, which he used while speaking inside a room, was well modulated, somewhat resembling a twenty-mile gale of wind. The second voice, which he used while working outside, reminded me of a well-developed thunderstorm. The third voice he used for his cussing and swearing. I will not try to describe this voice for fear of setting fire to my paper. Seven times during my association with Paul Bunyan did I hear him use that third voice, and six of the seven times his hot words set forest fires raging, fires which took 50 men about a week to extinguish. For that reason all men refrained from antagonizing him.

"Strangely, I was not afraid of Paul. His size meant nothing to me. A camp cook feared no man, for the simple reason that all men feared the camp cook. Make no mistake, my friends. Every lumber-jack knew who buttered his bread; therefore, the cook had nothing to fear from any man, big or small. I was supreme in my cookshack.

"I invited Paul Bunyan into the cookshack, and he accepted with alacrity. We had fine talks, and he amused me greatly with stories of his exploits and feats of strength. He was very hungry and a wee bit tired, though he would not admit the latter. No true lumberjack ever would admit that he was tired.

"During our conversation Paul explained that he had walked from Marquette, a town on Lake Superior which was discovered by a priest of the same name, which sounded to me like a queer coincidence. I often intended asking Paul whether the priest or the town arrived there first, but the thought escaped me at the proper moment.

"But here was Paul, and he was hungry. And was Paul hungry? I'll tell the cockeyed world he was. I had a crew of twenty-two men in the cookshack, and I put them all to work preparing food for our distinguished guest. To this day you probably will hear some old woods cook tell how he was there when I fed Paul Bunyan his first meal in the Lower Peninsula. But pay no heed to such tales. All of my helpers are dead, have been for forty years. I am the lone survivor of that eventful day, so you will have to take my word for the menu that was served to Paul.

"We worked for three hours to prepare the meal. It consisted of 33 pounds of beef, 1 whole venison, 2 bushels of fried potatoes, 12 loaves of bread, each weighing 4 pounds, 7 gallons of coffee, 6 hams, 12 dozen eggs, 678 pancakes made with exactly 1 barrel of buckwheat flour, topped off with 6 gallons of pure maple syrup. Paul Bunyan was hungry.

"He stayed with us for three months; I was sorry to see the big feller go when he made up his mind to leave us. I could write all night on some of the great things which our camp accomplished while he was in our midst, but I fear you would not appreciate the tales I would tell. And to be frank with you, I sometimes doubt them myself.

"Don't make the mistake that many readers of Paul Bunyan tales have made. Most of the stuff and nonsense which has been written about him has been deliberate lies. What I write is authentic and truthful, as I am the only man living who knew Paul,

Personally,
Joe Muffreau."

It may surprise the reader to hear that Paul Bunyan had two brothers. The middle brother was Soar Bunyan, a hulk of a woodsman who liked his "strong stuff." James W. Clapp of Pontiac remembered Soar very well. Parks Allen of Ithaca thought he had met Soar Bunyan while tramping around James Bay.

This middle Bunyan started to make his own brew. While carrying a bottle of this powerful liquor in his pocket, somewhere north of Parallel 49, the cork popped out. He grabbed for the falling bottle, but it slipped from his grasp and was shattered. A big hole was burned in the earth's surface. Slowly it filled with water until it was full; it has since been named Lake Superior. The splash and the overflow formed the other Great Lakes. What trickled away made the St. Lawrence River.

It may have been Soar Bunyan who dragged his pick as he went westward into the Pacific woods and made the Grand Canyon. Some storytellers insist that Paul made the Grand Canyon and not Soar.

George Hedquist of Menominee and Detroit and Perry Allen of Shepherd have told the story of the labors of the youngest of the Bunyan boys, Cal S. Bunyan. Cal S. built the most wondrous railroad in the world: the Ireland, Jerusalem, Australian and Southern Michigan railroad. Cal got the idea after Jim Hill finished building the Great Northern. The Bunyans are ambitious people and would not be outdone by Jim Hill.

"It took the largest steel mill in the country two years," said Swede Hedquist, "operating on a schedule of a 36-hour day and a 9-day week, to produce one rail for Cal. Each tie was made from an entire redwood tree. Finally, the train was finished; it had 700 cars. It was so long that the conductor rode on a twin-cylinder, super de luxe motorcycle to check tickets. He punched each ticket by shooting holes through it with a 45-calibre automatic.

"In the dining car a whole beef was used for each meat serving. Two cement mixers were required to stir the gravy. Potatoes were lifted out of the frying pans with steam shovels. A tank car full of yellow cream was coupled in front of each diner to furnish cream for the coffee.

"The train went so fast that after it was brought to a dead stop it was still making 65 miles an hour. After two months of service, the schedule had been speeded up so that the train arrived at its destination an hour before it left its starting point.

"One day Cal S. said to the engineer, Peter Peterson, 'Peter, give her all the snuss she's got.' That was the end of the I., J., A., and S. M. railroad. The train traveled so fast that friction melted the steel rails and burned the ties to ashes.

"On the last half-mile of the line, where the track has a steep up-grade, the train was making such speed that when it reached the top of the grade the engine took off just like an airplane and carried itself and the 700 cars so far into the stratosphere that the law of gravity quit working.

"That was years and years ago, but the I., J., A., and S. M. is still rushing through space, probably making overnight jumps between stars, by Jupiter."

THE SHANTY BOY'S LIFE

CHAPTER II

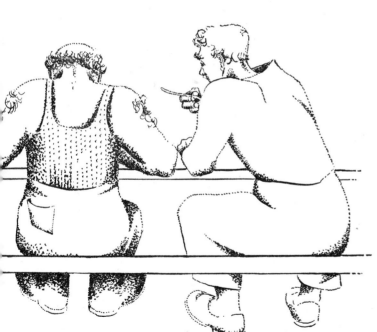

Entertainment in the lumber camps was not only storytelling, but also included singing, fiddling, and dancing. The 1872-73 daybook of Charles Turner of Saginaw Valley fame has evidence that shows the shanty boys liked their musical entertainment: Twelve men in a lumber camp were charged thirty-two cents each as a "share in a fiddle." I wonder who played that fiddle; it was probably someone like Fred Arlt of Summit City, Empire Stites of Barker Creek, Kelly Rogers of Alden, Ernie Losey of Thompsonville, Leon May of Fife Lake, Carl Lathrop of Pleasant Valley, Frank Hufford of Breckenridge, Frank Lyons of Barryton, Silver Jack Swan of Gladstone, Benno Hoffmeier of Wheeler, Grant Little of Wellston, or Fred Powell of Elk Rapids.

Most folklorists seem to have agreed that the dulcimer is an instrument of the Appalachians and the Ozarks. The mistake is theirs. The lumber camps of the Great Lakes boasted some excellent dulcimer players. These men made their own instruments and kept them in repair. The dulcimer was the piano of the north woods. The Michigan Lumberjacks, a well-known band of woods entertainers who played some good professional shows from St. Louis to New York, have had four notable dulcimer players: Art Mulford, colorful little cricket from St. Louis, Michigan; Sam Rouse, sober-faced soloist from Wheeler; Jay Mudge, beloved entertainer from Kewadin; and Don Baker, nimble-fingered accompanist from Ithaca. Besides these four, as many others have helped from time to time: A. O. Fish, southpaw whanger from Mt. Pleasant; Elgia Hickock, loose-string artist from Sears; Bob Spinner, the speed kid from Elk Rapids; and Jack Benford, musical nephew of Jay Mudge. Others like Brooks of Midland, Borkhorst of Kingsley, and Cross of Lodi, Wisconsin, have reputations on the instrument.

Dancers were many. Without women in camp, the shanty boys made a "woman" out of a man by the simple process of tying a handkerchief about the arm. Such "women" made second-rate partners, though, at the stag dances. The solo dancers did the buck-and-wing, jig, and "stomp." The "stomp," which takes as much energy and agility as the Cossack dance, has brought applause for Bob Hockaday of Molasses River, Bob Losey of Thompsonville, Bill McBride of Isabella City, Calvin Thomas of Jennings, Billy Girard of Gladstone, and Foxy Grandpa Hufford of Breckenridge. Old Perry Allen jigged with the best of them when nearly ninety. Lyle Mackenzie of Alma is a master buck-and-winger well past the eighty mark; Henry Babcock of Alma and Frank Scribner of West Branch were nearly as good.

THE JOLLY SHANTY BOY

The American lumberjack, like other robust frontiersmen, had ample self-confidence. The Mike Finks of the keelboatmen, the roughnecks of the oilfields, the sourdoughs in the goldfields, the buffalo skinners of the short grass country, and the lumberjacks of the pinewoods could boast, but the "big brag" had better make good his boast.

The rollicking bravado of *The Jolly Shanty Boy* was not uncommon in Bangor, Saginaw, Muskegon, Marinette, Eau Claire, Cloquet.

I first heard this verse from Peter Mahon of Deerfield Center. Afterwards I heard it from John Wilson of Gladwin, Alf Levely of Edenville, Bill McBride of Isabella City, Ernie Losey of Thompsonville, Jack Kelly of Empire, Tom Jones of Manistee, Jay Mudge of Kewadin.

Other collectors like John Lomax and Louise Pound have known the same piece arranged for other occupations.

1   I am a jolly shanty boy
    Who loves to sing and dance.
I wonder what my girls would say
    If they could see my pants!

2   With fourteen patches on the knee
    And six upon the stern,
I'll wear them while I'm in the woods,
    And home when I return.

3   For I am on my jolly way
    I spend my money free.
I have plenty—come and drink
    Lager beer with me.

4   I'll write my love a letter,
    I'll give the ink a tip,
And if that don't fetch her up to time,
    I guess I'll let her slip.

5   For I don't care for rich or poor,
        I'm not for strife or grief;
    I'm ragged, fat, and lousy, and
        As tough as Spanish beef.

6   Those dark-eyed single lasses,
        They think a heap of me.
    You ought to see me throw myself
        When I go on a spree,

7   Rigged up like a clipper ship
        Sailing round the Horn,
    Head and tail up like a steer
        Rushing through the corn.

8   Now to conclude and finish,
        I hope I've offended none.
    I've told you of my troubles
        Since the day that I begun,

9   With patched-up clothes and rubber boots
        And mud up to the knees,
    With lice as big as chili beans
        Fighting with the fleas.

It seems that almost every lumberjack knows the alphabet song. I have heard it in the Pacific Northwest, in the St. Regis long-leaf forests north of Pensacola, among W. T. Neal lumber workers near Brewton, Alabama, around Berlin, New Hampshire, and, of course, in the Great Lakes area.

The choruses differ somewhat. I know these variations:

"Give a shanty boy grub (pork, whiskey) and nothing goes wrong"

"It's a shanty boy's right and nothing goes wrong"

"If your shanty boy's well, there's nothing goes wrong"

"Fare the shanty boys well, and there's nothing goes wrong."

These varying chorus lines came from David D. Smith of Whittemore, Michael Sullivan of Mt. Pleasant, Hiram Taylor of Standish, L. M. Converse of Buchanan, Peerless Grice of Marion, Mrs. William Garchow of Farwell, and Mrs. Bertha O'Shea of Boyne City.

Thomas J. Smith of Gordonville sings "Hi-derry-dong."

ALPHABET SONG

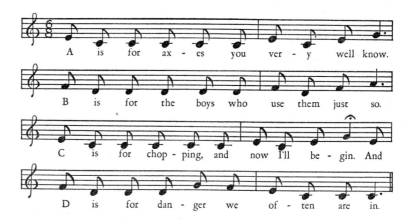

1   A is for axes you very well know.
    B is for the boys who use them just so.
    C is for chopping, and now I'll begin.   And
    D is for danger we often are in.

Chorus
    So happy, so happy, so happy are we,
    No mortals on earth are as joyful as we.
    Hi-derry-hi, hi-derry-down,
    Give a shanty boy grub and there's nothing goes
        wrong.

Logs were marked with the "iron" mentioned under "I." The "jobber" for "J" contracts to get out lumber for the owner.

The first version is one sung by Art Murray of Mio, Allen Coy of Pentwater, William Butler of Standish, William McKinstry of Frankfort, Wes Hurley of Croswell, Nelson Santhony of Pinnebog, Charles Woodruff of Belding, and Margaret Little of Rosebush. Norman Anning of Ann Arbor learned the words from his teamster father in Gray County, Ontario, with a "more tuneful tune."

2 E is for echoes that through the woods ring.
   F is for foreman, the head of the thing.
   G is for grindstone, so swift does it turn. And
   H is for handle, from elm you will learn.

3 I is for iron to mark the pine's end.
   J is for jobber who no money can lend.
   K is the keen edge our axes do keep. And
   L is for lice that work while you sleep.

4 M is for moss we stag our camp with.
   N is for needle we patch our pants with.
   O is for owl that hoots in the night. And
   P is the pine that always falls right.

5 Q is for quarrels we never allow.
   R is the river our logs they do plow.
   S is for sleigh so stout and so strong. And
   T is for teams to haul them along.

6 U is the use we put our teams to.
   V is for valley we haul our logs through.
   W is for woods we leave in the spring.
   Now I've ended my song; no more will I sing.

The second version is also widely known. Upper Peninsula shanty boys like Gerhard Green of Nahma, C. M. Scully of L'Anse, Art LaRue of Eckermann, "Smokey" Thackman of the Soo, Billy Girard of Gladstone know the piece. These words actually came from Jerry A. Archambeault of St. Louis and John Gregory of Applegate.

1   A is for the articles that we always need.
      B is for the bunks; in the bunks we do sleep.
      C is for the crabs that bite us all night.
      D is for the devils that keep up the fight.

Chorus
    So merry, so merry, so merry are we,
    Not a mortal on earth is so merry as we.
    Hey-derry! Ho-derry! Hey-derry-down!
    Give a shanty boy whiskey and nothing goes wrong.

2   E is for the earnings for the work we have done.
      F is for fire that keeps us all warm.
      G is for grease we fry our cakes in.
      H is for horses that haul the logs in.

3   I is for ice on the roads all along.
      J is for jugs that knock us all down.
      K is for kanthooks we roll our logs with.
      L is for legs that make us step quick.

4   M is for manners we often forget.
      N is for neatness as well as the rest.
      O is for oleo we eat on our bread.
      P is for poles that hold up our bed.

5   Q is for quick we all ought to be.
R is for rum that puts us to sleep.
S is for stove we all sit around.
T is for teamster a-singing this song.

6   U is for union of lumberjacks strong.
V is for vanish: our camps are now gone.
W is for wilds we always lived in.
X as in oxen who skid the logs in.

7   Y is for yodel that calls the men in.
Z is for zero that makes us all think.
And this is the song we all like to sing.
Just before the break in the spring.

Henry Dodge, the author of this poem, spent his boyhood on a farm southwest of Watrousville in Tuscola County, Michigan. Later he moved to the county seat of Caro. Dodge won quite a local reputation as a maker of popular verses.

THE OLD RIVER DRIVER

1   I hired out at Saginaw
        To work with Avery's men.
  'Twas on the north branch of the Cass
        That they were lumbering then.

"Bud's" was the Buddington Hotel in Watrousville. The Avery from Saginaw was a big operator; Sewell Avery, late president of Montgomery Ward and United States Gypsum, was of this Avery family.

Mike Toohey, who loves to recite poetry, recited this one.

2   'Twas a weary tramp to reach the camp,
    The road a line of mud.
First night we stayed in Watrousville,
    Of course, we stopped with "Bud."

3   Bud's place that night was crowded full.
    We camped upon the floor.
And of his best we took it straight
    And poured it down galore.

4   Next morn we took a drink for luck
    And started on our way.
We reached the town of Centerville
    At ten o'clock that day.

5   'Twas at Cross Tavern where we stopped
    And early dinner had.
Of course, we took a few more drinks
    To make our hearts feel glad.

6   Then we poured some whisky in our boots
    To help our gallded feet.
Then on up towards the Forks we went
    To Ren Teachout's retreat.

The historian will do well to visit the Bay City library and read the *Lumberman's Gazette*. Albert Miller in 1873 wrote in that magazine that he and Isaac Butterfield "purchased from Joshua Davis the pine on eighty acres of land situated near the Cass River, a mile or two below Tuscola Village, for which we gave one hundred dollars, and I think it was as fine a lot of pine timber as I ever saw. The purchase date was 1846. . . . The first logs of any amount that were run down the Cass River, to be manufactured on the Saginaw, were cut in the winter of 1846-47."

Albert and Richard Miller, Sewell Avery, Curt Emerson, James Tolbert were among the Cass operators. Tolbert was a bachelor who made his home at the Bancroft Hotel. Curt Emerson was the character who just about ruined the opening of the Bancroft,

DRIVING LOGS ON THE CASS

1   Come all you river drivers, wherever you may be,
That's standin' round the fire tonight, come listen unto me,
While I relate the dangers and the hardships that we pass
While driving logs for Miller on the winding River Cass.

2   It was early in the season ere the winter's ice and snow
Began for to diminish and the streams began to flow,
When Miller's logs went pounding from off the river's side
And started on their voyage 'way down the sweeping tide.

3   'Twas in the early morning before the sun rose in the sky
Lotus, our foreman, would come around, and "Daybreak" was his cry.
Cold, wet, and hungry we'd roll out into the frosty air;
And soon in haste we would partake of the all too scanty fare.

coming uninvited to the banquet and kicking a lot of dishes onto some pretty gowns.

Ruth Craig of Marquette collected this ballad from sources other than Mrs. Agnes Briggs of Birch Run and Jay Smith of Traverse City. Mrs. Briggs got the words from her grandfather; Jay Smith remembered them from the Wright and Ketchum camps, with the teakettle logmark.

4   Although we know that Miller had provided for his
       men
    The best the country could afford and had it with them
       then,
    We scarce could get enough to eat, and what we did,
       I own,
    Was never more than half prepared. 'Twas then we
       thought of home.

5   'Twas all the fault of Old Black Joe, our dirty greasy
       cook;
    For fixing up the grub for us no pains at all he took.
    Hot biscuits were nothing but raw dough and heavy
       as stone;
    And ofttimes we had to make a meal of them alone.

6   The most of them were young men who worked at
       this employ;
    The most of them were young men whose hearts were
       filled with joy.
    And often when the jam ahead was broken with a
       cheer
    It was heard the whole length of the drive and answered by the rear.

7 Although we were detained by some of Raynard's
   crew
 Who tried their best to hold our rear and force a
   passage through,
 As our brave boys came flocking up to assist those in
   the rear
 'Twas then they began to scatter, thinking some danger near.

8 At length with joy we reached the forks and halted
   for the night.
 The drive we had been following lay plainly in our
   sight,
 All grounded on the rapids a little space below;
 And for the want of water no farther could we go.

9 'Twas in the morn that Miller saw that they were thus
   detained.
 With sorrow he discharged the crew; not even one
   remained.
 All for Cass City we were bound ere homeward we
   would start,
 To take a glass in friendship before that we would
   part.

10 Arguing at George Tennant's house, the drinks went
   freely round.
 The boys were all in merriment; the barroom did
   resound.
 As our foreman did not try our feelings for to mar
 As each made his appearance he was hoisted o'er the
   bar.

11 A few hours were briefly spent, and then the word
   "Good-by"
 We heard from almost every man as night was draw-
   ing nigh.
 Thus gay as summer flowers we all left Miller's drive,
 Happy to think through dangers wild we all were yet
   alive.

Snagging was the work of river drivers in the rear of the log drive, releasing the logs caught on sand bars, rocks, and other cursed obstructions. Klacking Creek flows through the Ogemaw Hills east of Houghton Lake. There was some good timber in that area.

The colorful Fred Scribner of West Branch sing-songed this one.

The Chippewa River of Michigan runs from Coldwater Lake and empties into the Tittabawassee River near Midland. It is one of several streams of the once heavily timbered Saginaw basin.

Mrs. Jennie Railling of Brant told me: "This song was composed by a boy from New York for Charlie Turner in the winter of 1871 and was handed down to me." Bradley, Turner and Company had several camps up the rivers from Sanford. Daybooks of Charles Turner in 1872 and 1873

SNAGGIN' THE KLACKIN'

Hip-fa-lad-di-dey!
Hip-fa-lad-di-dey!
Greybacks, they
   Are mighty thick.
A dollar a day
Is all they pay
For snaggin'
   The Klackin' Crick.

TURNER'S CAMP ON THE CHIPPEWA

1   Come all you jolly lumbermen
     That do a-lumbering go,
  Come listen to my story,
     Which I relate to you,

2   Of the hardships and the dangers
     We undergo each day
  While working up in Turner's camp
     On the banks of the Chippewa.

show such lumberjack names as Baker, Buchanan, Bullock, Crimons, Culbert, Cullin, Garmon, Hawkins, Hopkins, Sandbrook, Smith, Stevenson, Young; it would seem that Turner's men came from the British Isles. The charges these lumberjacks incurred, as shown in the daybooks, were largely "1 plug of tobacco — 50 cents." Charles Turner was still operating in 1885, for I have a Western Union telegram dated March 16, 1885, from the village of Sanford to Charles Turner, reading: "Your logs are on fire. We have sent up some men. Thomas Moore."

Isaac Fancher, Mt. Pleasant, said the Stoney Brook Camp, eight miles above Mt. Pleasant, was owned by Henry Winesburgh.

This song was known to Dan Carey of Mt. Pleasant, Tom White of Houghton Lake, James Stanley of Farwell, Perry Allen of Shepherd. Rex Stowe of Gladstone has a stanza he remembered, a stanza that sounds as if it came from Wisconsin:

It was down the logging stream,
    Down along the Chippeway,
There's a silent grave that's visited
    By drivers on the way.

3   I started out from Saginaw,
        The weather being fair,
    And fetched up at eleven o'clock
        At a little place called Clare.

4   The place it was so stumpy
        I thought it must be Hell;
    So I jumped aboard of Skanker Stage
        And rode into Isabelle.

5   While bumping around Isabelle
        I thought I'd go to work
    Away up in the lumber woods,
        Where there's no time to shirk.

6   So I started after dinner
        For to take a little tramp,
    And fetched up just at suppertime
        In Charlie Turner's camp.

7   At five o'clock next morning
        The cook his horn did blow
    To call the boys to eat their hash
        So to the woods they'd go.

The songs mentioned in stanza 14 can be found in this volume. This version came from Bill McBride of Isabella City.

8   At first they put me sawing,
        But found it did not pay;
So when the boys from Quebec quit,
        They sent me to load the dray.

9   While loading of that damned old dray,
        Of course I was so green,
Such piling up of top logs
        Before I'd never seen.

10   The driver being in a hurry
        For to get over his route,
It was lift a log and roll a log
        And cant a log about.

11   When the last log was loaded,
        To the river we did go;
The way we made those horses climb
        You bet it was not slow.

12   To see him driving on the road
        You'd swear that he was drunk,
For he never was known to make a trip
        But he hung up on a stump.

13 When the last load was on the dray
   To the shanty we would go,
 Where the boys would tell us of the things
   That happened years ago.

14 Some would sing of Johnnie Troy
   And some of the "Cumberland" crew,
 But of all the songs, that I liked best
   Was of bold Jack Donohue.

15 The boys were glad when Sunday came,
   That they might have a rest;
 Some would go a-visiting
   All dressed up in their best;

16 Some would gather round the caboose,
   And more would grind the axe;
 Some would mend up their old clothes,
   And more their old shoepacks.

17 It was on the first of April
   The birds began to sing;
 We began to break the rollways,
   So I thought it must be spring.

18 But the boss came up from Saginaw
   And looked over the books
  And said, "My boys, you'll have to stay
   Two more weeks on Stoney Brook."

19 Now the winter, it is over,
   Our work it is done;
  We will all go down to Saginaw
   And have a little fun.

20 Some will go on Skanker Stage,
   And more will take the train.
  If you get there before I do,
   It's whoop-er-up, Liza Jane.

According to M. E. McGaugh in *Settlement of the Saginaw Basin,* as late as 1888 Saginaw and Bay City shipped 1,349,315,000 board feet of lumber besides shingles.

Isaac A. Fancher in his address delivered

JOHNNY CARROLL'S CAMP

1 One evening in November
   I happened for to stray
  To Johnny Carroll's lumber camp
   On the banks of the Chippewa.

in Mt. Pleasant on July 4, 1876, reported that in 1874 Isabella County had "number of sawmills, 11, 6 steam and 5 water power, employing 91 men . . . cutting 7,738,000 feet of lumber valued at $120,174. Also 4 shingle mills cutting $33,398 worth of shingles."

Carroll is pronounced Carl by the lumberjacks. In fact, it is still pronounced Carl by the old-timers of the Chippewa watershed.

R. C. M. Gardiner of Lansing, John Watson of Rosebush, Henry Babcock of Alma, and John Waddington of Farwell knew this song besides these from Mt. Pleasant: Isaac Fancher, Dan Carey, Verna Campbell. This is another Bill McBride version.

2 With him I tried to grub and chop
   And level down the road,
 To make ready for the winter's snow
   On which our logs are towed.

3 With grub hoes, pries, and axes
   We loosed the roots and stumps
 And filled up all the hollows
   As we leveled down the lumps.

4 Now to be a perfect woodsman
   And to learn the lumbering trade,
 You must spend a certain length of time
   A-toiling on the grade.

5 Now choppers, grind your axes,
   And sawyers, file your saws,
 And teamsters, mend your harnesses,
   For these are lumbering laws.

6 The blacksmith and the tinker,
   They mend our tools so neat;
 You cannot fear the work, brave boys,
   Our tools are all complete.

7   Our cooks they are good-natured,
        So we get the best of food;
    We get the best variety
        The country can afford:

8   Potatoes, apples, turnips, beans,
        And syrup, pure and sweet.
    Although we have no appetite
        We cannot help but eat.

9   There's bread and biscuits, pies and cookies,
        All seasoned to our taste;
    And our cook he is so careful
        That nothing goes to waste.

10   Our sleeping camp is well arranged
        With bunks so wide and deep;
    And as night upon us reaches
        We quickly go to sleep.

11   The choreboy in the morning
        Gets up and builds the fire,
    And keeps our camp so clean and neat
        We cannot but admire.

12 You ought to see us working
   As the weather's mild and fine,
 With canthooks, axes, peaveys,
   How we work the stately pine.

13 From daylight on till dark, brave boys,
   We toil from day to day
 A-working in the pinewoods
   On the banks of the Chippewa.

14 When winter 'tis all over,
   And our lumbering too is done,
 We'll get out on the river, boys,
   And there we'll have some fun.

15 We'll start our logs a-floating
   And drive them down the stream.
 And before we go for home, brave boys,
   We'll sing the lumbering theme.

Leota on the Muskegon River was once important in the lumber business. The old-timers mention lumber barons like W. S. Gerrish, D. F. Comstock, and O. P. Pillsbury, who had connections there.

John Lang of Clare, who recited this for me, was schooled at Dodge, once a village of 500 and now only a memory. It had been a camp of Dodge and Barnes. George Lewis of Leota knew this verse but Denton "Cripe" Bailey of Harrison furnished this version.

WAY UP AT LEOTA

1 Come all you jackpine savages,
   Wherever you may be,
And listen to a story
   I will relate to thee.
I'll tell you all the hardships
   That come to us each day
While working for John Griffin
   Way up at Le-o-ta.

2 The teams nearly froze to death—
   At least the drivers say—
With slivers for their bedding
   And jackpine boughs for hay.
The camp lets in the moonshine
   By night, and the sun by day.
The men they almost freeze to death—
   At least, that's what they say.

3 At four o'clock each morning
   Or somewhere there about,
You hear Old John a-hollering,
   "Roll out, my boys, roll out!"

The breakfast is at five o'clock;
    And it's getting to be a fright,
With taters and salt for breakfast
    And cold bouillon at night.

4   The loads are loaded too heavy,
    The teamsters always say.
With four-foot drifts upon the road
    And eight-foot bunks on the sleigh,
They make their trips though just the same.
    There's Billie, George, and Joe.
And if they can't get through the drifts
    They have to make a tow.

5   Now, if we ever get out of here,
    I'll tell you what we'll do,
That is, if we ever do survive
    And live the winter through:
We'll revive our constitutions
    With whiskey and good cheer,
And return again to the jackpines
    At the first of another year.

The story of a lumberjack coming into Boyne City or Grayling or Frederic or Hillman on the narrow gauge is a recurring one. He has always taken over the caboose in O'Connor manner, has broken furniture, and has built a fire in the middle of the car. When the train stops, he puts up quite a fight. These goings-on are interesting enough, but to ride "two giant spruces . . . standing straddled" down the chutes is truly a feat to be celebrated in song.

Jack O'Leary of Nessen City and John Robertson of Hubbardston furnished this version.

WHEN O'CONNOR DREW HIS PAY

1   When O'Connor drew his pay,
  Though he drew it miles away,
The people of the city felt
  The shock of it, they say.

2   He rode two giant spruces
  Through the smother of the chutes;
He rode them standing straddled,
  Shod and spurred in spike-soled boots.

3   When O'Connor reached the city,
  He reached it with a jar;
He had all the cushions burning
  In the middle of the car.

4   When at last they got him cornered,
  They had rung in three alarms.
It took the whole department
  To tie his legs and arms.

5   They took him to the limbo.
  Right and left along the line,
He pulled his roll and willingly
  Kept peeling off his fine.

6   They sold his heavy mackinaw
            And they sold his spike-soled boots
    For enough to pay his freightage
            Back to Rapparora Chutes.

7   They took him to the station,
            And they shipped him back by freight.
    To begin a year of chopping
            In township number eight.

8   And earnestly he swore
            As they dumped him on the shore,
    He'd never spent his savings
            So pleasurably before.

GRIZZLY HOGAN

Elmore Vincent, "the Northwest Shanty Boy," has included in his song pamphlet *Grizzly Hogan* about as it is sung by George Hedquist of Detroit. I first heard it from Billie Theade of Miles City, Montana; he had picked it up in Spokane.

1   Oh, there's a road to Seattle
            As plain as can be;
    And if you want to see a wreck
            Just take a look at me.

2   For I've been to Seattle
        And drunk a little beer.
    I take my fun where I find it
        And come back again next year.

3   Oh, when I go to Seattle,
        The cops are in despair;
    For when I'm tight and feelin' right
        Just for a helluva tear

4   There's not a cop in fifty
        Who dares to stir a hair.
    They call me Grizzly Hogan;
        I'm the son of a grizzly bear.

5   Oh, I cut down two trees at once,
        A big one with each hand,
    And throw them trees a good ten miles
        And catch them when they land.

6   I eat tobacco by the plug
        And drink my whiskey clear.
    They call me Grizzly Hogan;
        I'm the son of a grizzly bear.

7   Once I had a sweetheart,
       But I don't have her now.
   I kissed her when I left her,
       And it broke her lower jaw.

8   I patted her back gently,
       And broke the three ribs there.
   They call me Grizzly Hogan;
       I'm the son of a grizzly bear.

CAMP 13 ON THE MANISTEE

John Fleming of Bellaire furnished this
Camp 13, Jay Mudge of Kewadin had
heard it.

1   As husky a bunch as ever was seen
   War the lumberin' crew of Camp Thirteen,
   Each one a hard-boiled piece o' meat
   Who'd just as soon any time fight as eat;
   Stage always set for a jambouree
   At Camp Thirteen, on the Manistee.

2   But they all went 'way back, and set down
   An' behaved, when Sam put his war paint on.

Sam war the blacksmith, big an' strong
As the iron he pounded all day long.
He had cleaned the clocks o' most o' the crew,
An' of several strangers passing through,
And all considered he had the goods
On any man in the northern woods.
So whatever Sam'l opined, it went
In Camp Thirteen, or else it meant
A fight, and few indeed were they
Who wouldn't crawfish, 'n' back away,
When Sam concluded—quite frequent, too—
To change the map of some of the crew.
A beetle-browed bully he war 'n' mean,
An' as dirty a fighter as ever war seen.

3 Jim war a trapper who shacked on the Pine
Where lay most of his trappin' line;
From down East some'ere war hinted at,
Woods for 'is health—somethin' like that,
A sort of professor, some of them said,
'Way up in figgers, 'n' damn well read;
Not there very long, nor so very well known,
Lived in 'is dugout all alone,

Come through the camp 'most every day,
Sober 'n' quiet, not much to say,
But work in the woods?—couldn't hire 'im to,
Huntin' 'n' trappin' war all he'd do.
So, as you may imagine, he wa'n't ace-high
In Camp Thirteen, an' when he'd swing by
With traps 'n' gunny sack, axe, 'n' gun,
The taunts, 'n' gibes, 'n' insults flung
By Sam the blacksmith war simply a fright.
Sam done it on purpose to pick a fight;
But Jim he'd grin 'n' go right on
An' never say nuthin' to anyone.
So the boys set 'im down for a coward, 'n' few,
If any, his friends in that lumberin' crew.
But they changed their minds one rainy day,
An' changed 'em sudden, I'm here to say,
For on that day, to the boys' surprise,
Jim put on a show that opened their eyes.

4   The day had been rainy, a little too damp,
So most o' the boys war a-loungin' in camp,
An' frequently hittin' the bottle—the way
They always had done on a rainy day—
Sam had been rushin' the growler, too,

An' that meant trouble as most of 'em knew,
For when half-tanked, 'twar his delight
To paste some sucker 'n' make 'im fight.
Or, he'd misstate anything, so I've heard,
Just to see who dared to dispute his word,
Then beat up on 'im; and on that day
He war startin' out in the same old way,
War already ugly, 'n' darin' to fight—
A sign he'd been hittin' 'er up all right.

5   At the instant he war expoundin' his creed
An' glarin' 'round to see who disagreed.
Then he lit into Christ, 'n' sorry to tell,
Raked 'im fore 'n' aft to a fare-ye-well,
'Mid nods of approval, howls of applause,
The slappin' o' thighs, 'n' loud guffaws,
An' Sam war still a-rossin' of him,
When the shack door opened an' in walked Jim,
Wet as the one lone rat in the sack
Slung like a turkey to 'is back.

6   He listened a minit to what Sam said,
Then: "Talk like that 'bout a man that's dead!
I'll say right here afore the crew

It shows you're yaller through 'n' through.
Why, if Christ war here, you ornery cur,
He'd lick you so quick you'd be nowhere;
You're just a bully, a low-down brute,
An' a dirty, stinkin' liar, to boot."

7   The men turned ashen. They held their breath,
For to call Sam a liar was courtin' death.
He'd started somethin', Jim had, all right,
For "liar" in Camp Thirteen meant "fight."
An' he fight with Sam! The boys all knew
To the dot exactly what Sam would do.
Some wag in the crowd suggested that
Jim select the place to be buried at.

8   Sam stood for a minit in blank surprise,
Then murder shot from his beadlike eyes.
An' the hate of a demon shook 'is frame.
He turned to the crew: "Bob, take 'is name,
An' his age, 'n' what relatives of his.
Them things all go at the obsequies.
This here young feller's wantin' to fight,
I opine he'll be missin' from home tonight.
So just plant 'is carcass somewhere near

An' inform 'is friends, if he has any here;
I've too much respect for the fish, you see,
Or I'd dump the remains in the Manistee.
Free to admit I ain't got the gall
To up 'n' deliberate pisen 'em all.
Sorry, boys, that it's gotta be done,
But come on out 'n' witness the fun."

9   Of course, the boys, they all turned out
An' formed a ring to witness the bout.
Most all opinin' that right from the go
Jim wouldn't have the ghost of a show,
But all stood mute, 'n' nary a one
Opened his trap when the fight begun,
For all well knew that Sam would trim
Any an' all who cheered for Jim,
An' that he'd be next without a doubt,
Who hollered for Jim if Sam won out.
Plain as the nose on your face, it showed
That Sam had the whole crew buffaloed.

10   When the men they squared 'n' Sam he led,
The boys figgered Jim war as good as dead;
But they soon discovered, Sam did too,

That he'd bit off more'n what he could chew.
An' when he clinched 'n' war throwed so hard
An' so slick and quick that the camp war jarred,
Then the boys give tongue (for all could see
That Sam wasn't in it nor never would be).
Then it dawned on him he had somethin' to do
Or be licked to a frazzle, one of the two.
He'd discovered, sudden, that Trapper Jim
War a Tartar to handle 'n' too much for him,
An' that this 'ere fight would either pave
His path to glory or to the grave.
But for him to be trimmed by this trapper bloke,
An' afore the crew! Why, he'd rather croak
For it meant his finish, plain to be seen,
As cock o' the walk in Camp Thirteen.

11   The fight! Man alive, but it war a peach,
Both 'bout the same height, 'bout the same reach,
Sam heavier, stronger by far than Jim—
Jim more like a race hoss, trim 'n' slim,
But there wa'n't a thing he didn't know
'Bout the fightin' game, from pivot blow,
To counter, duck, sidestep, 'n' swing,
For a fight it war 'bout the classiest thing,

The boys all said they'd ever seen,
That fight that day at Camp Thirteen.

12 Sam seemed to know his rep war at stake,
An' that this 'ere fight would make or break,
So he fit like a tiger. Fumin' mad,
He'd swing with every ounce he had,
Miss by an inch; then rave 'n' swear,
Rush in frenzy, and fan the air.
While calm 'n' cool, Jim like a flash
Would sidestep Sam, 'n' land a smash
Square in the mush, or over the heart.
Hell! Sam war licked from the very start.
This rearin', swearin', fannin' the air,
Them things never git a man nowhere
'Cept out o' wind. Jim had 'er doped out,
Knowed every second what he war about,
Fit to the blueprint all the way,
An' boy, did he punish Sam that day!

13 Sam fit till he buckled 'n' went all in
From a beaut' of a left Jim hooked to the chin
That sent 'im reelin' senseless till he
Fell plunk in the icey Manistee.

The boys all hollered: "Let 'im drown,
We don't want the son of a gun aroun',"
An' drown he would, for he couldn't swim,
If it hadn't been for that same Jim,
Who shed 'is cruisers, made a dive,
An' brought Sam out more dead 'n alive.

14   Jim stood 'im on end 'n' dreaned 'im out,
Kicked 'is pants, 'n' rolled 'im about
Till Sam come to, then Jim, he said:
"Now never again speak ill of the dead."

15   What Sam had predicted come true all right,
Jim war missin' from home that night,
But the boys o' the camp war a-fetin' of him,
An' a-drinkin' health to the Trapper Jim.
An' tickled to death war that lumberin' crew,
When Blacksmith Sam met 'is Waterloo.

THE MANISTEE LUMBERJACK

Leon May of Fife Lake and Alma, one of the last of the best lumberjack entertainers, sang this song.

1   I'm a rippin', roarin' lumberjack
      From up on the Manistee
In town for the night to celebrate
      And the drinks are all on me.
It's in the top bunk I always sleep;
      Against the wind I spit,
Chew a pound of Peerless every day
      And never wear any mitts.

Chorus
    So set 'em up and drink 'em down.
      For all the drinks are free.
    For when this lumberjack comes to town,
      The drinks are all on me.

2   I've eaten pea soup in a French cookshack
      And beans with Jim McGee,
Stewed prunes in Thayer's and McCracken's camps
      And swallowed my breakfast at three.
I've worked on the big pines week after week,
      Drove wheels through the summer days.
I've tailed 'em down to the nine-foot bunks
      On the teamsters' logging sleighs.

3   The tote team's in from the camp tonight.
        Dead broke I'm going back.
Good-by to all you boys and girls,
        Good-by to all you jacks.
I'm going back to the lumber camp
        Way up on the Manistee,
And when the camp breaks up in the spring,
        Be looking out for me.

Chorus

    So I'll set 'em up and we'll drink 'em down
        Until our heads are sore;
And when my stake is all played out,
        I'll go back and earn some more.

Tread on my corns and tell me lies,
But don't feed me dried-apple pies.
There were not a few lumberjacks who got
awful tired of dried-apple pies and beans.
The Michigan lumberjacks were very fond
of what they call "the beans song." It is
sung to the modified tune of *Maryland, My
Maryland* with the shanty boy soloist singing the lines and the other jacks singing the
refrain. It seems well fitted to whiskey
tenors and beer basses.

Louis Sands was the big Scandinavian
who lumbered off millions of board feet
of pine in the Clam Lake (now Cadillac)
and Manistee regions. He was a huge man
who disregarded appearances. Once, while
driving his team to Cadillac, one horse died.
He pulled the horse alongside the trail, took
off the harness, threw most of the harness
in the wagon, and using just enough to
attach himself to the wagon, he came trot-
ting into Clam Lake teamed up with the
remaining horse. Though he was several
times a millionaire, he always looked like a
common laborer and generally acted like
one. He brought many Scandinavians into
middle Michigan. It is said that when the
Salvation Army lassie asked an immigrant

LOUIE SANDS AND JIM MC GEE

1   Who feeds us beans? Who feeds us tea?
        Louie Sands and Jim McGee.
    Who thinks that meat's a luxury?
        Louie Sands and Jim McGee.
    We make the big trees fall kersplash
    And hit the ground an awful smash;
    And for the logs who gets the cash?
        Louie Sands and Jim McGee.

2   Who feeds us beans until we're blue?
        Louie Sands and Jim McGee.
    Who thinks that nothing else will do?
        Louie Sands and Jim McGee.
    Who feeds us beans three times a day
    And gives us very little pay?
    Who feeds us beans, again I say?
        Louie Sands and Jim McGee.

3   Who gives us pay for just one drunk?
        Louie Sands and Jim McGee.
    When we hit the Manistee kerplunk—
        Louie Sands and Jim McGee.

Swede in New York, "Will you work for Jesus?" the Swede answered, "Ay tank ay rather vork for Louie Sands."

The version here is that sung by Frank Hufford of Breckenridge, Leon May of Fife Lake, Tom Jones of Manistee, Carl Lathrop of Pleasant Valley, and Bill McBride of Isabella City.

We drink our whisky and our ale
And sweep the town just like a gale;
Then who comes to get us out of jail?
    Louie Sands and Jim McGee.

4   Who feeds us beans each blessed day?
    Louie Sands and Jim McGee.
Who'll feed us beans on Judgment Day?
    Louie Sands and Jim McGee.
And when that judgment's passed, and we
Know just where they're going to be,
Who'll eat beans through eternity?
    Louie Sands and Jim McGee.

LITTLE BROWN BULLS

Franz Rickaby vouched for the popularity of *Little Brown Bulls* in Wisconsin. I myself know about its popularity in Michigan and Minnesota. I also heard it in Wisconsin from Henry Thompson and the jacks around

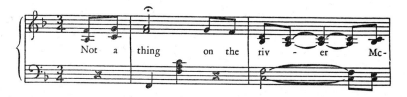

Not a thing on the riv - er Mc-

Phillips. Though R. P. Gray does not mention the song in *Songs and Ballads of Maine Lumberjacks*, I have heard it in both Maine and New Hampshire. In the summer of 1955 I heard it in the Northwest.

Art Goodenough of East Milbrook insists that this verse records a skidding match at Thayer Lumber Company near Fife Lake, Michigan.

Various singers have various names for the principals. Tommy Agan of Buckley, who "never went to school a minute" in his life, sings Paddy Golden instead of Bull Gordon. Leon May calls the swamper Kennebec John, Art Goodenough calls him Salisbury John, William Dashneau of Muir calls him Sandberry John, as did Ernie Losey of Alma.

The common-enough refrain was sung by the assembled jacks. This version is the Goodenough version.

1   Not a thing on the river McCluskey did fear
As he threw his goad o'er his big spotted steers.
They were tall, plump, and handsome, girted nine
     foot and three.
"By Gad," says McCluskey, "they're the laddies for
     me."

Chorus

    Derry-down-down-down, derry-down.

2   Then down came Bull Gordon; his skidding was full,
As he hollered, "Whoa hush," to his little brown bulls.
They were short, plump, and shaggy, girted six foot
     and nine.
"They're too light," says McCluskey, "to handle our
     pine."

3   Three logs to the thousand our contract did call;
The skidding was good and the timber was tall.
Says McCluskey to Gordon: "I'll make the day full,
I can skid two to one to your little brown bulls."

4   "No, no," said Bull Gordon, "that thing you can't do,
Though your big spotted steers are the pets of the crew.

And it's mark my words, laddie, you will find your
    hands full
If you skid one more log than my little brown bulls."

5   So the day it was set and it quickly drew nigh
When for twenty-five dollars and belt they did try.
All anxious and eager that morning they found
When the judges and scalers appeared on the ground.

6   First down came McCluskey with a whoop and a yell,
Saying, "Mind me, bold laddies, and chew your cuds
    well.
Keep a cud in each jaw for to keep your mouths full,
And it's easy to conquer the little brown bulls."

7   Next down came Bull Gordon with blood in his eye,
Saying, "This day I will conquer McCluskey or die."
Says Sandy, his swamper, "You need have no fear,
For it's easy to conquer the big spotted steers."

8   Oh, the sun it went down and the boss he did say,
"Hurrah, boys, Hurrah! it's enough for today."
And it's little they thought when Bull Gordon came
    down
That a hundred and forty he would put on the ground.

9   When supper was over McCluskey came on
For the twenty-five dollars and belt he had won.
"Hold on," said the scaler, "hold on for a while,
For Bull Gordon has beat you by nearly a mile.

10   "You have a hundred and ten and no more,
While Bull Gordon has beat you by ten and a score."
'Twas then that McCluskey did roar and did swear,
And he pulled out by handsfull his long yellow hair.

11   Says McCluskey to Gordon, "My money I'll pool,
And the belt you can have for your little brown bulls."
So here's to Bull Gordon and Sandberry John
For the biggest day's skidding on the river they'd done.

12   So it's fill up your glasses and fill them up full,
And we'll drink to the strength of the little brown bulls.

If the Bunyan stories keep growing as they seem certain to do, it is inevitable that Old Paul will have a wife and children. The wife Esther Shepherd found seems inadequate. I have already come to know Paul's brothers, Soar and Cal S.; Soar Bunyan was the middle one. Now, Fred Arlt of Summit City gives me a glimpse of Paul's daughter.

IN OLD PAUL BUNYAN'S CAMPS

1   Have you heard about Paul Bunyan's camps
Where they used moon and stars for lamps?
They worked about ten thousand men
In Old Paul Bunyan's camp.

2   The flunkey he was quite a man.
With hams on his feet he'd grease the pan,
The pan they mixed the pancakes in,
In Old Paul Bunyan's camp.

3   The wind jammer now and then
Brought the pancakes to the men.
The dough was mixed with feet and hands
In Old Paul Bunyan's camp.

4   It's funny how Paul Bunyan dressed.
He used basswood bark to make his vest;
For buttons he used big sawlogs,
In Old Paul Bunyan's camp.

5   His pants of maple and cedar both.
He used hemlock bark for an overcoat.
His teeth he picked with canthook stalks
In Old Paul Bunyan's camp.

6   Paul's only daughter went for a stroll.
She lost herself behind a knoll.
    She wandered into settled land.
        Far from Paul Bunyan's camp.

7   And there to her surprise she found
A man and team plowing the ground.
    It was something she had never seen
        Round Old Paul Bunyan's camp.

8   She took them in her apron deep
To show her father how they'd creep.
    They were more tender than the lice
        In Old Paul Bunyan's camp.

PAUL BUNYAN'S MANISTEE

In the Southwest I learned that Paul Bunyan dragged his canthook to form the Grand Canyon of the Colorado, though some insist that the dragging was done by Paul's middle brother, Soar. In Ontario I heard

1   Paul Bunyan, the lumberman, came from St. Paul.
He owned a big ox that was eleven feet tall.
He mowed down the trees as the farmers mow hay,
And the crew was at work before break of day.

74

of Paul's digging the St. Lawrence. Here in Michigan he dug the Muskegon according to Leon May and the Big Manistee according to W. J. Taylor of Bay City and Henry Jordell of Hoxeyville.

This is Taylor's version of the song, with the popular Irish chorus of "Down, down, hi-derry-down."

Chorus

Down, down, hi-derry-down.

2 I lived in Bay City; no work in sight;
My board bill was due, and I had to take flight.
My clothes they were torn; I was known as "the scamp."
It was poverty drove me to Paul Bunyan's camp.

3 I got to Paul Bunyan's that very same day,
Climbed up his barn and lay down in the hay.
With some Peerless tobacco I did my pipe tamp,
And I smoked away trouble at Paul Bunyan's camp.

4 When I got to the camp I asked for a job.
Paul Bunyan he met me with a wink and a nod.
My two eyes were black, and I looked like a tramp,
But he says, "You're right welcome to Paul Bunyan's camp."

5 They called me next morning before three o'clock:
"Get up, you old bum, and pull on your socks.
When you work for Paul Bunyan you don't sleep all day;
And you feed his big ox or you don't get your pay."

6   I went to the cookshack; 'twas forty rods long.
     We all commenced eating at the sound of the gong.
     We drank black coffee, ate the breast of a sow;
     The pancakes were turned with a big sidehill plow.

7   With a ham strapped to each foot a big black coon
     Greased that griddle from morning till noon.
     We had to eat pancakes twice every day,
     And at nine in the evening we rolled in the hay.

8   I went to a skidway the logs to roll down
     With a big Highland Hoosier that they called John Brown.
     He was big and was strong and was known as a champ,
     Was that hog-headed Hoosier at Paul Bunyan's camp.

9   The trees were all cut and lay on the ground;
     We needed a river to run the logs down.
     Paul's ox was a big one, of tons he weighed three,
     And he plowed a deep ditch for the Big Manistee.

10   Paul Bunyan quit logging when his muley ox died.
     He had a big tent made out of its hide.
     With the ox yoke for a pillow he smokes his big pipe
     And he dreams of the river he made in one night.

James McGillivray conceived the Round River yarn when his city editor at the *Detroit News–Tribune* told every member of the staff to write his own "good story" for the Sunday magazine. It appeared on July 24, 1910.

"My first knowledge of such a lumber-camp character as Paul Bunyan came to me," said McGillivray, "when I was scaling logs at the logging camp of Rory Frazer, 22 miles east of Grayling on the north branch of the Au Sable River. I was then 13 years old, but big like an adult man.

"Among the hardy bunch that constituted Rory's logging crew were such noted characters as Dutch Jake, a Hollander wag, but plenty tough; Pat O'Brien (POB), tougher than Jake; and Big Paddy Grant, who claimed that he was an orderly for General Grant.

"The men had a lounging shanty by themselves, removed from Rory's domicile, and hardly an evening went by that some lumberjack did not bring out some new angle on the prowess of a mythical Paul Bunyan."

ROUND RIVER DRIVE

1   'Twas 'sixty-four or 'sixty-five
     Yes, it was durin' the War,
     Or after that, or jis' before.
     Those were the days in Michigan—
     The good old days when any man
     Could cut and skid and log and haul
     And there was pine enough for all.

2   Then all a logger had to do
     Was find some timber that was new
     Beside a stream; he knew it ran
     To Huron or Lake Michigan,
     That at its mouth a mill there was
     To take the timber through its saws.
     In those old days the pioneer
     He did not read his title clear
     To mansions there or timber here.

3   Paul Bunyan! You have heard of Paul.
     He was the kingpin of them all—
     The greatest logger in the land.
     He had a kick in either hand
     And licked more men and drove more miles
     And got more drunk in more new styles

Though *Round River Drive* is the longest versification of Paul Bunyan material, it is not too long for lumberjack memories. A Mr. Wood, from Winn (formerly Dutchville), could recite the entire poem perfectly. Paddy McKay of Oscoda and A. G. Ellico of Bay City could do almost as well.

This versification of the McGillivray tale was done by Douglas Malloch. It was taken from the files of the *Midland Republican*.

Than any other peavey prince,
Before or then or ever since.
Paul Bunyan bossed that famous crew—
A bunch of fightin' bruisers too:
Black McDonald, Dirty Dan,
Dutch Jake, Red Murphy, Pat McCann,
Bad Silver Jack and One-eyed Ross—
Ten birlers from the Tittabawass—
Lads from Bay City, Saginaw—
Big Fournier, Tug-leg Bonefont—
And more that didn't give a damn,
The kind of men to break a jam,
Clean up a barroom, rastle rum,
Or give a ten-spot to a bum.

4   Paul Bunyan and that fightin' crew
In 'sixty-five or 'four or 'two,
They started out to find the pines
Without regard to section lines.
So north by west they made their way
A hundred miles, until one day
They found good timber on high land
And roarin' water right at hand.
They built a bunk- and cook-house there—

They didn't know exactly where,
And what is more, they didn't care.
Before the spring, I'll give my word,
Some mighty funny things occurred.

5   Now near the camp there was a spring—
Hot? It would steam like everything.
One day the chap that hauls supplies
Had on a load of mammoth size,
A load of peas. Just on the road
Beside the spring he ditched the load.
An' all those peas—the bloomin' mess—
Fell in the spring—a ton I guess.
He came to camp expecting he
Would get from Bunyan the G. B.
But Joe the cook, a French Canuck,
Said "Paul, I t'ink it ess ze luck,
An we will have ze grand bullion!"

6   To prove the teamster not at fault,
He took some pepper, pork, and salt—
A right proportion each of these—
And threw them in among the peas.
We had enough, and good soup, too,

To last us all the winter through.
The rest of us were kindo' glad
He split the peas, when soup we had—
But, gosh! the flunkies, they were mad—
Because each day they had to tramp
Three miles, and tote the soup to camp.

7   Joe had a stove—some furnace, too—
Right size for the Paul Bunyan crew.
Say what you will, it is the meat,
The pie and sinkers choppers eat
That get results. It is the beans
And spuds that are the best machines
For cuttin' Norway, skiddin' pine,
An' keepin' hemlock drives in line.

8   That stove of Joe's, it was a rig
Fer cookin' grub that was so big
It took a solid cord of wood
To start the fire a-goin' good.
The flunkies cleaned three forties bare
Each week to keep a fire in there.
That stove's dimensions, south and north,
And east, and westward, and so forth—

I don't remember, just exact,
An' I would hate to state a fact
Unless I knew that fact is true:
Fer I would hate deceivin' you.
But I remember once when Joe
Was puttin' in a bunch of dough—
And he then thought, at least he tried,
To get around the other side.
But long before the bend he turned,
That bread not only baked—it burned!
Joe had two coons for flunkies, Tom and Sam.
He used to strap a great big ham
Upon the foot of each of 'em.
When he made pancakes each A. M.
They'd skate around the stove lids for
An hour or so or maybe more,
And grease 'em for him. But one day
Old Pink-eye Martin—anyway
He couldn't see so very good—

9   Old Pink-eye, he misunderstood
Which was the baking-powder can,
And in the dough four fingers ran
Of powder—blastin' powder—black!

Those niggers never did come back!
He waited for a week or so,
But never found them—
That, you know,
It was the year of the blue snow.
We put one hundred million feet
On skids that winter. "Hard to beat"—
You say it was? That was some crew.
We took it all off one forty, too.
A hundred million feet we skid—
That forty was a pyramid.
It runs up skyward to a peak;
To see the top would take a week—
The top of that, it seems to me,
Was far as twenty men could see.
But down below the logs were slides,
For here was pine on all four sides.

10   One day we see some deer tracks there—
Bigger'n any of a bear.
Old Rory Frazer, straw boss, on
The side those deer tracks was upon,
He didn't say so much, but he
Thinks out a scheme, an' him an' me,

We sets a key log in the pile—
Watches that night for quite a while;
And when those deer come down to drink,
We tripped that key log in a wink.
We killed two hundred in that herd,
For Rory's scheme was sure a bird;
Enough of venison we got
To last all winter, with one shot.

11   Paul Bunyan had the biggest steer
That ever was in camp, that year.
Nine horses he'd out-pulled on skid—
He weighed five thousand pounds, he did.
The barn boss—handy man, besides—
Made him a harness from the hides
Of all those deer—it took 'em all.
Old Pink-eye Martin used to haul
His stovewood in. Remember yet,
How buckskin stretches when it's wet?
One day when he was haulin' wood—
A dead pine that was dry and good—
One cloudy day, it started in
To rainin' like the very sin.
Old Pink-eye pounded on that ox

And driv him over roads and rocks
To camp. He landed there all right,
Then turned around—no log in sight!
But down the road, around the bend,
Those tugs were stretchin' without end.
Well, Pink-eye, he goes in to eat;
The sun comes out with lots of heat—
It dries that buckskin that was damp
And hauls that log right into camp!

12   That was a pretty lucky crew!
An' yet we had some hard luck, too.
You've heard of Phalen, double-jawed?
He had two sets of teeth that chawed
Through almost anything. One night
He sure did use those molars right.
While walking in his sleep he hit
The filer's rack, and after it
Then with the stone trough he collides—
Which makes him sore and mad besides.
And long before he gets his wits
He chaws that grindstone into bits.
And yet, we didn't miss it so,
For to the top we used to go,

An' from that forty's highest crown
We'd start big stones a-rollin' down.
We'd lay an axe on every one
An' follow it upon the run—
Before we'd reach the lower ledge
Each axe, it had a razor edge.

13 Jim Liverpool, one day he bet
Across the river he could get
By jumpin', an' he won it, too,
And got the laugh on half the crew,
For twic't in air he stops an' humps,
And makes the river in three jumps.

14 We didn't have much booze around,
Fer every feller that we found
An' sent to town fer applejack
He'd drink it all up comin' back.

15 One day the bull cook, parin' spuds,
He hears a sizzlin' in the suds.
And finds the peelin's, strange to say,
Is all fermentin' where they lay.

16   Now Sour-faced Murphy in the door
       Was standin', and the face he wore
       Convinced the first assistant cook
       That Murphy soured 'em with his look.
       And when they had the peelin's drained
       A quart of Irish booze remained.

17   The bull cook told the tale to Paul;
       And Paul took Murphy off the haul
       And gave him—very willingly—
       A job as camp distillery.

18   At last, a hundred million in,
       'Twas time for drivin' to begin.
       We broke the rollways in a rush,
       And started through the rain and slush
       To drive that hundred million down
       Until we reached some sawmill town.
       We didn't know the river's name,
       Nor where to someone's mill it came,
       But figured that, without a doubt,
       To some good town 'twould bring us out,
       If we observed the usual plan
       And drove the way the river ran.

19 Well, after we had driven for
  A week or so or maybe more
  We came across a pyramid
  That looked just like our forty did.

20 Two weeks again; another, too.
  What looked like our camp come in view.

21 Then Bunyan called us all ashore
  And called a council like of war.
  Says Paul, "With all this lumbering
  Our logs won't bring us a damned thing."
  The next day after, Silver Jim,
  He had the wits scared out o' him,
  For while he's breakin' of a jam,
  He comes on the remains of Sam—
  One coon who made the big ascent
  And through the cookhouse ceilin' went
  And Pink-eye grabbed the fatal tin
  And put the blastin' powder in.
  And we realized at last
  That every camp that we had passed
  Was ours. Yes, 'twas then we found
  The river we was on was round,

And though we'd driven many a mile
We'd driv a circle all the while.

22   And that's the truth as I'm alive
About the great Round River drive.
What's that? Did ever anyone
Come on that camp of 'sixty-one
Or 'sixty-three or 'sixty-five,
The year we drove Round River drive?
Yes, Robert Rayburn, Pete and me,
T. Hanson, and some two or three
Of good and faithful gentlemen
Came on that famous camp again
In west of Grayling several miles,
Where all the face of Nature smiles.
We found the place in 'eighty-four;
But it had changed some since the War.
The fire had run, some summer, through
And spoiled the logs and timber, too.
The sun had dried the river clean,
But still its bed was plainly seen;
And so we knew it was the place,
For of the past we found some trace:
The jew's-harp Tom could play so well,

A peavey with a Circle L—
For that, you know, was Bunyan's mark.
The hour was late; 'twas gettin' dark.
We eastward went—a corner found
And took another look around.
Round River, so we learned that day,
On Section Thirty-seven lay.

Two of the better known lumberjacks of this country were Jigger Jones and Silver Jack. Jigger Jones was a Maine man, Silver Jack was a Michigander. Herbert Nolan in *Camp Sixteeners* (1939) has a picture of Silver Jack. Nolan states that Silver Jack Driscoll was born in Lynsay, Ontario. "He was 6 feet 2 inches tall and weighed 210 pounds stripped . . . he was a foul fighter . . . and would kick a man any place he could with his corked boots."

LUMBERJACK'S REVIVAL OR RELIGION IN CAMP

1 I was on the drive in 'eighty
      Working under Silver Jack,
Which the same is now in Jackson
      And ain't soon expected back.

2 There was a chump among us
      By the name of Robert Waite,
Kind of slick and cute and tonguey,
      Guess he was a graduate.

The prison records show that Driscoll served two terms in Jackson. He was first received at Michigan State Prison, Jackson, as Number 175 on February 26, 1873, from Saginaw County on a charge of robbery. He gave his occupation as river driver. He was discharged May 5, 1877. Again he was received July 15, 1880, as Number 2425. He gave his age as 29. He was sent up from Saginaw County on a charge of robbery. On October 25, 1889, he was pardoned by Governor Luce. John Schuch of Saginaw, John McIsaac of Manistique, formerly a Saginaw policeman, and T. G. Belanger of L'Anse, whose mother ran the hotel where Jack died, insist that for the latter crime at least, Jack was framed while under the influence of liquor.

Silver Jack's battles with Curley LeClair, Jack McGovern, Al Hartenstein, and Joe Fournier have become legend. Though some insist that Jack never fought the thick-skulled Frenchman Fournier, Jack Fathey of Midland swore he saw the fight. He said Joe tried to butt Jack into submission but caught one of Jack's powerful uppercuts. Edward Loud of Au Sable said that Jack fought a bare-fisted two-hour draw with the Pere Marquette brakeman, Al Hartenstein. Harry B. Smith of Bay City has a

3   He could gab on any subject
        From the Bible down to Hoyle,
    And his words flowed out so easy,
        Just as smooth and slick as oil.

4   He was what they called a skeptic,
        And he loved to sit and weave
    Highfalutin' stories
        Telling what he didn't believe.

5   One day while we were waitin'
        For the flood to clear the ground,
    We all sat smoking niggerhead
        And hearing Bob expound.

6   "Hell," he said, "is all a humbug."
        And he showed as clear as day
    That the Bible was a fable,
        And we 'lowed it looked that way.

7   Miracles and suchlike
        Was too thin for him to stand;
    And for Him they called the Savior,
        Why, he's just a common man.

photograph of Joe Fournier, who he says lost the "championship of the Saginaw valley" to Silver Jack at Red Keg. Walter A. Henry of Saginaw saw Silver Jack win over Blinker Robertson on the "L. G. Mason." H. R. McKinstry of Big Rapids tells of the fight in the Evart Saloon between Silver Jack and Jack McGovern: after an hour of bare-fist fighting McGovern admitted defeat and accepted Jack's supremacy on the Muskegon.

There are legends about Silver Jack's being shot in an Upper Peninsula train, being killed in a Ewen saloon, being drowned in the Tahquamenon River, or drifting to an unknown end in the Washington redwoods. Both John I. Bellaire of Manistique and T. G. Belanger of L'Anse know that the real Silver Jack is buried in L'Anse. "He died with his boots off, in the Ottawa Hotel, in L'Anse, Michigan, April 1, 1895," declared Belanger. "Beside him under the pillow of his bed were found the following: a bottle of cough medicine, $85 in bills, and a note: 'This will be enough to bury me.' Silver Jack came to L'Anse in 1893, probably from Seney. Seney at that time was one of the wildest and wooliest towns in Michigan."

8 "You're a liar!" someone shouted,
  "And you got to take it back!"
Then everybody started;
  'Twas the voice of Silver Jack.

9 He chucked his fists together,
  And he shucked his coat and cried,
" 'Twas by that there religion
  That my mother lived and died.

10 "And although I ain't always
  Used the Lord exactly right,
When I hear a chump abuse him,
  He must eat his words or fight."

11 Now this Bob he weren't no coward,
  And he answered bold and free,
"Stack your duds and cut your capers,
  For there ain't no flies on me."

12 They fought for forty minutes,
  And the lads would hoot and cheer
When Jack spit out a tooth or two
  Or Bobby lost an ear.

Amos Buck of Grand Rapids and Houghton Lake vows he heard this song on the Au Sable as early as 1895. Vean Barber of Mesick, Chris Petersen of Yuma, Clare Allen of Kalkaska, Ernie Losey of Thompsonville, Edward Loud of Oscoda, and Mrs. Minnie Sias of Midland say the tune was *My Darling Clementine*. James Slingerlend of Morley first sang me this version. The one here came from Edward Loud as recorded by the Gibbs sisters.

13   But Jack kept on reasonin' with him
            Till the cuss begin to yell,
    And Bob 'lowed he'd been mistaken
            In his views concerning Hell.

14   Then Jack he got Bob under
            And he slugged him onc't or twic't,
    And Bob confessed almighty quick
            The divinity of Christ.

15   So the fierce discussion ended,
            And they rose up from the ground.
    Someone brought a bottle out
            And kindly passed it round.

16   And they drank to Jack's religion
            In a quiet sort of way,
    And the spread of infidelity
            Was checked in camp that day.

The song called *Shanty Boys in the Pine* is known by a variety of names: *Jim Lockwood's Camp, McLaughlin's Shanty, Jim Murphy's Camp, Porter's Camp, Francisco's Camp, Gilbert's Camp, Robbins' Hotel, Robertson's Camp, Pete Lilly's Shanty.*

The first version with camp name varied was sung by Walter Avery of Cadillac, Wes Inman of Midland, George Morrison of Saginaw, Belle Smock of Ithaca, David D. Smith of Whittemore, Thomas Webster of Tawas City, Manson and George Marsh of Mio, and Cassie Davison of Farwell.

SHANTY BOYS IN THE PINE

1   Now boys, if you will listen
        I'll sing for you a song.
    It's all about the pinewoods
        And how to get along.
    They are a jolly set of boys,
        So merry and so fine,
    Who spend the pleasant winters
        A-cutting down the pine.

2 When falltime rolls around,
   Great will be the day;
Some will stay close at home,
   Others wander far away.
The farmer and the sailor,
   Likewise mechanics too—
It takes all kinds of tradesmen
   To compose a lumber crew.

3 The choppers and the sawyers,
   They lay the timber low.
The skidders and the swampers,
   They haul it to and fro.
Then there come the loaders
   Before the break of day:
"Load up the teams, my boys,
   And to the river haste away."

4 When noontime it rolls around,
   The foreman loudly screams,
"Down with your tools, my boys,
   And haste to pork and beans."
Arriving at the shanty,
   The music then begins:

The rattling of the water pail
>And the banging of the tins.

5　"Hurry you up, my bully boys,
>You Tom, Dick, Jim, and Joe,
Or you will have to take the pail
>And for the water go."
You ought to see them jump and run
>When the cook his horn does blow,
For it ain't like any of the boys
>To miss their hash, you know.

6　Dinner being over,
>To the shanty they will go.
They all load up their pipes and smoke
>Till everything looks blue.
"It's time for the woods, my boys,"
>The foreman he will say.
They gather up their hats and mitts
>And to the woods they haste away.

7　They all go out with cheerful hearts
>And well-contented minds,

For the winter winds do not blow cold
    Among the waving pines.
And merrily their axes ring
    Until the sun goes down.
Hurray, boys! Our day's work's done!
    For the shanty we are bound.

8   Boot packs and rubbers
    Are laid all to one side;
Socks and rags and gloves and mitts
    Are all hung up and dried.
And supper being ready,
    They all arise to go—
It's not the style of the shanty boy
    To miss his hash, you know.

9   At four o'clock in the morning
    The choreboy will loudly shout,
"Roll over, all you teamsters,
    It's time that you were out."
The teamsters then they will get up
    All in a rush and say,
"I cannot find my boot packs,
    And my socks have gone astray."

10 The choppers they will then get up;
   Their socks they cannot find.
 They lay it to the teamsters
   And cuss them till they're blind.
 They jump and sing and dance and shout
   To pass away the time,
 To pass away the lonely hours
   While working in the pine.

11 When springtime rolls around
   The foreman he will say,
 "Down with your tools, my boys,
   And haste to break away."
 And when the floating ice is gone,
   Business it will thrive,
 Two hundred able-bodied men
   Are wanted on the drive.

12 With jam pikes and with peaveys
   These brave men nobly go
 To risk their own dear lives, my boys,
   On Muskegon River-O.
 On cold and frosty mornings
   When shivering with the cold,

There's so much ice upon my jam pike
 That I can scarcely hold.

13 Now boys, wherever you hear this song
  You'll find these words are true,
And if you are inclined to doubt
  Inquire of the lumber crew.
For 'twas in Jim Murphy's shanty
  This song was sung with glee.
And boys, remember when you hear this song,
  Remember L. D. C.

This second version with camp name varied was known by W. H. Shafer of Tustin, Ira Simons of Ashton, William Sheldon of Vestaburg, Tom Shurtz of Kalkaska, Teal Hogan of Hubbardston, George Barnett of Branch, Preston Kuhn of Stanwood, Mrs. Louise Jackson of Atlanta.

1 Come all you jolly fellows
  And listen to my song;
It's all about the pinewoods boys
  And how they got along.

2 They are a jolly set of lads,
  So jovial and fine,
That spend a pleasant winter
  A-cutting down the pine.

3   The choppers and the sawyers
        Will lay the timber low.
    The swampers and the skidders
        Will haul it to and fro.

4   Then down will come the teamsters (loaders)
        Before the break of day.
    They all load up their sleighs (teams)
        And for the river haste away.

5   Noontime rolls around;
        The foreman loudly screams,
    "Lay down your saws and axes
        And come for pork and beans!"

6   We arrive at the shanty,
        And the splashing then begins;
    There's rattling of the water pails
        And banging of the tins.

7   Then you hurry up there,
        You Jack or Bill or Joe.
    You must take the water pail
        And for some water go.

8   While he is after water
        For dinner then they cry.
You ought to see us run and jump
        For fear we'll lose our pie.

9   When dinner is all over,
        We to the shanty go,
And all fill up our pipes and smoke
        Till everything is blue.

10   "It's time for the woods, my boys,"
        Our foreman he will say.
We all pick up our hats and mitts;
        To the woods we haste away.

11   Oh! it's loudly do our axes ring
        Until the sun goes down.
Then it's hurry up, my boys,
        We're for the shanty bound.

12   We arrive at the shanty
        With wet and cold feet,
And all pull off our boot packs,
        For supper we must eat.

13 The horn blows for supper;
        We all arise and go.
    It's not the style of any of us
        To miss his hash, you know.

14 When supper is all over,
        We to our shanty go
    And all smoke up our pipes again
        Till everything looks blue.

15 The boots, the packs, and rubbers
        Are all flung to one side;
    The socks and rags and mitts
        Are all hung up and dried.

16 At nine o'clock or thereabouts
        We to our bunks will climb
    To dream away the wintry night
        Among the waving pine.

17 At four o'clock next morning
        The foreman loudly shouts,
    "Hurry there, you teamsters!
        It's time that you were out."

18   The teamsters then arise
        In a frightened sort of way.
    "Oh, say, where are my boot packs?
        My socks have gone astray."

19   The rest of the boys then get up,
        Their rags and socks can't find.
    They lay it to the teamsters
        And curse them till they're blind.

20   One claims his socks are gone;
        He don't know what to do.
    Another claims his packs are lost,
        And he is ruined too.

21   Spring will soon be here, my boys,
        And bright will be the day.
    "Lay down your saws and axes, boys,
        And help to break the way."

22   The floating ice will soon be gone
        And business it will thrive.
    Five hundred able-bodied men,
        Are wanted on the drive.

23   With hand-pikes and with peaveys
        The boys will nobly go
And risk their manly lives
        On the raging river-o.

24   The cold and frosty morning,
        We shivering with the cold,
Makes so much ice on our jam pikes
        We can scarcely hang a-hold.

25   Now, some folks may laugh
        And think this is not true.
If they doubt a single word,
        See the men in Lockwood's crew.

26   For in Jim Lockwood's shanty
        This song was sung with glee.
This is the end of the shanty song
        Composed by C. C. C.
[That was composed by three (by me)]

A SHANTY MAN'S LIFE

The lumberjack of yesteryear sometimes liked to talk about the rigors of his life. These jacks even lacked "ale, wine, or beer." Jack Kelly of Empire says it in a couplet: "Along came the stage with a jug of good gin,/And that will have to do until the stage comes again."

They had good or bad food depending on the cook. There were no "pretty, fair maids" to be seen until the spring drive. Clothes were frequently damp and not infrequently wet.

This composition was rather widely known. This is the version of William Sheldon and Nels Plude.

1   A shanty man's life is a drearisome life,
        Though sometimes 'tis free from all care.
'Tis swinging an axe from morning till night
        In the midst of the forest so drear.
                'Tis the swinging an axe from morning till night
            In the midst of the forest so drear.

2   We are lying in the shanty; it's bleak and it's cold,
        While cold, wintry winds do blow.
The wolves and the owls with their terrible growls
        Disturb us from our midnight dreams.
                The wolves and the owls with their terrible growls
            Disturb us from our midnight dreams.

3   Transported we are from all pretty, fair maids.
        There's no whiskey seen till it's spring.
There's not a friend near to wipe away a tear
        While sorrow a sad mind will bring.
                There's not a friend near to wipe away a tear
            While sorrow a sad mind will bring.

4 Had we ale, wine, or beer, our spirits to cheer
  While here in the woods the long while,
Or a glass of anything while here all alone
  To cheer up our long, long exile.
   Or a glass of anything while here all alone
   To cheer up our long, long exile.

5 About four o'clock our noisy little cook
  Cries, "Boys, it is the break of day."
With heavy sighs from slumber we rise
  To go with the bright morning star.
   With heavy sighs from slumber we rise
   To go with the bright morning star.

6 When springtime comes in, double troubles begin,
  For the water it is piercing cold.
Dripping wet are our clothes and we're almost froze,
  And our pike poles we scarcely can hold.
   Dripping wet are our clothes and we're al-
   most froze,
   And our pike poles we scarcely can hold.

7 You can talk about your farms, but your shanty boy
  has charms;
  They are far superior to all.
They will join each other's hearts until death them all
  parts
  Whether they be great or small.
    They will join each other's hearts until
     death them all parts
    Whether they be great or small.

8 So rafting I'll give o'er and anchored safe on shore
  Lead a quiet and a sober life;
No more will I roam but contented stay at home
  With a smiling and a charming little wife.
    No more will I roam but contented stay at
     home
    With a smiling and a charming little wife.

There is a Maine song recalled by Mrs. Elizabeth Vermette of Mt. Morris from which this Michigan song doubtless descended. Mrs. Vermette recalls the first stanza:

> Come all you sons of freedom
>   From the gallant state of Maine,
> Come all you gallant lumberjacks
>   And listen to my strain.
> Upon the old Penobscot,
>   Where the rapid waters flow,
> We'll range the wildwoods over
>   And once more a-lumbering go.

Some of the old-timers call it *On The Tittabawassee*. The version here came from Ferdinand McCrary of Hope.

ONCE MORE A-LUMBERING GO

1   Come all you sons of freedom
>   That run the Saginaw stream,
> Come all you roving lumber boys,
>   And listen to my theme.
> We'll cross the Tittabawassee,
>   Where the mighty waters flow,
> And we'll range the wildwoods over
>   And once more a-lumbering go.

Chorus
> And once more a-lumbering go.
> And we'll range the wildwoods over
> And once more a-lumbering go.

2   When the white frost takes the valley,
>   And the snow conceals the woods,
> Each farmer has enough to do
>   To earn the family food.
> With the week no better pastime
>   Than to hunt the buck and doe,
> And we'll range the wildwoods over
>   And once more a-lumbering go.

Come all you sons of free-dom That
run the Sag-i-naw stream, Come all you rov-ing
lum-ber boys, And lis-ten to my
theme. We'll cross the Tit-ta-ba-was-see, Where the
might-y wa-ters flow, And we'll
range the wild-woods o-ver And once
Chorus
more a-lum-ber-ing go. And once
more a-lum-ber-ing go. And we'll range the wild-woods
o-ver And once more a-lum-ber-ing go.

3   You may talk about your farms,
        Your houses and fine ways,
And pity us poor shanty boys
        While dashing in our sleighs;
While round a good campfire at night
        We'll sing while the wild winds blow,
And we'll range the wildwoods over
        And once more a-lumbering go.

4   With our axes on our shoulders
        We'll make the woods resound,
And many a tall and stately tree
        Will come tumbling to the ground.
With our axes on our shoulders,
        To our boot tops deep in snow,
And we'll range the wildwoods over
        And once more a-lumbering go.

5   When navigation opens,
        And the waters run so free,
We'll drive our logs to Saginaw,
        Then haste our girls to see.
They will welcome our return,
        And we'll in raptures flow;
And we'll stay with them through summer
        And once more a-lumbering go.

Chorus
>And once more a-lumbering go.
>And we'll stay with them through summer
>And once more a-lumbering go.

6   When our youthful days are ended,
>>And our jokes are getting long,
>We'll take us each a little wife
>>And settle on a farm.
>We'll have enough to eat and drink,
>>Contented we will go;
>And we'll tell our wives of our hard times
>>And no more a-lumbering go.

Chorus
>And no more a-lumbering go.
>We'll tell our wives of our hard times
>And no more a-lumbering go.

MICHIGAN-I-O

There are many "I-O" and "I-A" folk songs; folklorists disagree as to the origin and importance of the various versions. *Michigan-I-O* is the best known from this area.

1   Come all you jolly lumbermen,
>>Wherever you may be,
>I pray you pay attention
>>And listen unto me.

Colonel Henry Shoemaker of Altoona,
Pennsylvania, has written that he collected
Michigan-I-O as *The Jolly Lumberman*
from Leary Miller while that lumberjack
was driving him from Cammal's Camp on
Lick Run to Lock Haven, January 2, 1901.
The colonel says that the "preacher of the
gospel" in the song was the preacher-lum-
berman, Rev. James Carrier of Lock Haven,
Pennsylvania.

Franz Rickaby collected a fragment of
Michigan-I-O from Arthur Milloy of
Omemee, North Dakota. Ottis Turpenning,
raw-boned riverman from Sumner, knew
more than one version. Warren Ackley of
St. Johns furnished this one.

'Tis of some jolly lumbermen
   Who did agree to go
And spend the winter pleasantly
   In Michigan-I-O.

2 'Twas early in the season,
   The fall of 'sixty-three,
A preacher of the gospel
   One morning came to me.
Said he, "My brisk young fellow,
   How would you like to go
And spend a winter pleasantly
   In Michigan-I-O?"

3 Then I made him this reply
   And unto him did say,
"My going out to Michigan
   Depends upon the pay.
If you will pay good wages
   And passage to and fro,
I think I'll go along with you
   To Michigan-I-O."

4   'Twas by this kind persuasion
         That he hired quite a train,
    Twenty-five or thirty,
         Both young and able men.
    We had a pleasant voyage,
         The way we had to go,
    And we landed safe in Saginaw
         In Michigan-I-O.

5   But here our pleasures ended,
         And troubles they began.
    Payne and Wright's agents
         They came a-sailing in
    And led us to a country—
         The way I do not know—
    Up the Tobacco River
         In Michigan-I-O.

6   To tell how we did suffer
         Is beyond the art of man;
    To give a fair description
         I'll do the best I can:
    Our board the dogs would laugh at;
         Our bed it was the snow.

God grant there is no meaner place
    Than Michigan-I-O.

7   But now the winter's ended,
        And homeward we are bound;
And in this cursed country
        No longer we'll be found.
We'll go back to our sweethearts,
        Tell others not to go
To a God-forsaken country
        Called Michigan-I-O.

Tom Knight of Houghton Lake is primarily responsible for this second version of *Michigan-I-O*. It is almost identical with that sung by Allen F. Smith of Newaygo, C. E. "Dad" Wright of Marinette, and C. A. Dedrick of Bay City. Tom Dunn of Gladwin uses the first version, merely changing "Payne and Wright's agents" to "Spencer and his agent"; he also said that a preacher of the gospel is "an agent who recruits labor for the lumber companies."

1   On the twenty-third of November
        In eighteen eighty-nine
There was Dan Monroe and his foreman,
        If I do rightly mind.
Said they, "My jovial fellows,
        Wouldn't you like to go
And spend the winter pleasantly
        In Michigan-I-O?"

2   We quickly did give answer
        And unto them did say,

George Barnett of Branch, Michigan, uses
this first stanza:

It was early in the season
  In the fall of '63
A preacher of the gospel
  Said unto me,
Said he, "My clever fellow,
  How would you like to go
And spend the winter pleasantly
  In Michigan-I-O?"

His sixth stanza is this:

Our joys now are over
  And our hardships then began.
To tell what we did suffer
  Is beyond the art of man.
Our food the dogs would laugh at;
  Our beds were on the snow.
God grant there is no worse place
  Than Michigan-I-O.

"This going out to Michigan
  Depends upon the pay.
If you give us good wages,
  Pay passage to and fro,
We might agree and go with you
  To Michigan-I-O."

3 They said they would give good wages
    And pay our passage out
Providing we'd sign papers
    To stay with them the route.
"But if you get homesick
    And home you have to go,
We cannot pay your passage
    From Michigan-I-O.

4 "And if you are not satisfied
    And do not want to stay
We do not want to bind you
    For one single day.
Just hand us back our money, boys,
    We gave to you, you know,
And you can leave that charming place
    Called Michigan-I-O."

Some Maine man must have brought the following stanza to Michigan. It was sung in the Saginaw valley by men like Bill McBride, Perry Allen, Art Mulford, and Clarence McClean.

> I've hearn of your Penobscot
>   Way down in parts of Maine
> Where timber grows aplenty
>   But hardly any grain.
> And I have hearn of Quaddy
>   And the Piscataqua;
> But they can't hold a candle
>   To Michigan-I-A.

5
> According to agreement
>   We got aboard the train;
> There were from twenty-five to thirty
>   Able-bodied men.
> We had a pleasant passage,
>   The route we had to go,
> Till we landed in headquarters
>   In Michigan-I-O.

6
> But now our pleasure ended,
>   And sorrow did begin.
> There was Dan Monroe and his foreman
>   Like the deuce came running in.
> But Dan Monroe and his foreman
>   Have met their match I know
> From the boys that came from Canada
>   To Michigan-I-O.

7
> Our bodies are hard as iron;
>   Our hearts are cased with steel;
> And hardships of one winter
>   Can never make us yield.
> They took us out across the land
>   To where we did not know,

Among the gambling Dutchmen
    In Michigan-I-O.

8   Now to describe this Michigan
      Is beyond the art of man,
But I'll try my endeavor
      And do the best I can.
The land is poor I'm very sure;
      The people are mean, you know.
And we cursed the day that ever we came
      To Michigan-I-O.

9   Now spring is returning,
      And homeward we are bound,
And in this cursed Michigan
      We'll never more be found.
We'll go and see our wives and sweethearts
      And tell others not to go
To this God-forsaken miserable place
      Called Michigan-I-O.

The old maps show that Michigan was thought to be a land of swamps. Corduroy roads were built across the swamps by laying logs side by side. The rambling lumberjacks who traveled these roads carried their extra duds in a "turkey," which was a bandana or a sack.

The *Detroit Free Press* has said that this "poem" was written in 1848 but that the author is unknown. G. W. Holland had it pasted in a scrapbook and dated 1849. This is the Holland version.

DON'T COME TO MICHIGAN

1   Come eastern friend, if you'll attend
Unto the counsel of a friend.
        I think it would be your best plan
        To stay away from Michigan.

2   The sawmills, they are dangerous things,
Are running fast and slabs they fling;
        They kill you or cut off your hand
        And leave you a beggar in Michigan.

3   Each Saturday night you want your pay,
Expect your money right away;
        But a written order is put in your hand.
        That's the way you're paid in Michigan.

4   The doctors, they are young in skill;
They do no good but put in their bill.
        They tell you they do all they can,
        And let you die in Michigan.

5   The people, they are getting sad
Because their money is all bad.

The banks all broke, but two or three,
And they'll soon die with cholerie.

6   The swamps, they are all filled with brakes
And are alive with rattlesnakes.
They lie and watch; do all they can
To bite the folks in Michigan.

7   There are a few nice boys, 'tis true,
But, oh alas, what can they do?
For if one wants a pretty wife,
She can't be found to save his life.

8   There are nice girls, I'll own it's true.
But, deary me, what can they do?
For if they want a decent man,
They have to leave their Michigan.

Bob Freeman of Harrietta, Ben Latham of Cadillac, Alvin Royce of Luzerne, Charles Ostrander of Roscommon, and Armand Keller of Kalkaska know this second version. It was furnished by Mrs. C. A. Welch of Harrison.

1   Come all young men, and you attend
And listen to the counsel of a friend.
If ever you seek another land
Don't ever come to Michigan.

2 We have big swamps covered with brakes,
And they're alive with rattlesnakes.
They lie awake, do all they can
To bite the folks of Michigan.

3 We have fine girls, I own 'tis true,
But, alas, poor things, what can they do?
For if they want an honest man
He can't be found in Michigan.

4 We have sawmills all o'er the land;
They saw lumber with a band;
They'll take your leg or take your hand
And leave you crippled in Michigan.

5 Our lumber camps are all so nice;
They're filled, the bunks, with bugs and lice,
You'll scratch and dig them with your hands,
But you still have them in Michigan.

6 Our roads are built of corduroy,
And if you travel very far
You sweat and swear and curse and damn—
That's how you travel in Michigan.

7   There's the doctor, and he'll tell
Great stories of his calomel,
Of the great doses that you must take;
'Twill cure your fever there's no mistake.

8   And then before you're out of bed
The doctor'll come, poke in his head,
"Some twenty dollars you must pay,
And I want my money this very day."

9   And there's the merchants I 'most forgot,
The biggest rascals in all the lot,
Who lie and cheat, do all they can
To keep you poor in Michigan.

10   And now my story I've told to you,
And if you'd find that it is true
Just pack your turkey as fast as you can
And come to live in Michigan.

Pete Petersen, the lumberjack turned novelist, had a few things to say about the chuck the lumberjacks ate, or refused to eat. Of course, food wasn't the best even in some cities, as is seen in a little ballad about the Pontiac Hotel that starts:

> There's a layout down in Pontiac,
>   They call it a hotel.
> The liver and hash is on second floor.
>   They cook it down in hell.

Pete has a version of Pontiac Hotel, but he has a better version about food in the woods.

DRILL YE TERRIERS

1   Oh, their filthy chuck we cannot eat,
Skippery cheese and rotten meat.
      They bake their bread and bake it well.
      They bake it harder than the hubs of hell.
Drill, ye terriers, drill.

2   Oh, the boarding boss went out one day
To get some sugar to put in our tay.
      He went out and found that sugar was dear,
      So he makes us drink our coffee clear.
Drill, ye terriers, drill.

3   Drill, ye heroes.   Drill all day.
For you'll drill all day
      With no sugar for your tay
      When you work for Breen and Holliday.
Drill, ye terriers, drill.

Though you might be as "safe with a lumberjack as if you were in God's pocket," as Jack O'Leary of Nessen City insists, the jack certainly did have a rough-and-tough reputation.

J. A. Gilfoy of Bay City said this tune is *My Name Is Solomon Levi*. The words came from M. E. Bearinger of Bay City.

I'M A SAGINAW VALLEY MAN

1   My name is Solomon Harmless
         From this world both wide and wild.
     I'm a regular mule in harness.
         I'm a wildcat when I'm riled.

2   I'm a Buffalo Bill, by jingo!
         All the way from hell, by damn!
     I'm not much on the lingo;
         I'm a Saginaw Valley man.

REVEILLE IN THE WOODS

Every lumberjack in the Great Lakes area knows "Get up, you lazy lumberjack. There's daylight in the swamp." Many a sleepy swamper and chopper has pulled on his damp woolen socks after being roused with "daylight in the swamp."

At Twining in the Au Gres valley Joseph Janiski recited this one.

        Beans are on the table.
        Daylight's in the swamp.
        You lazy lumberjack,
        Ain't you ever gettin' up?

NOW I LAY ME

This is a version of a prayer not unknown to the shanty boys; it was furnished by Delbert LaLone of Standish.

Now I lay me down to sleep
Where the lice and bedbugs creep.
If I should die before I wake,
Who in hell will blow my stake?

LUMBERJACK'S PRAYER

Mrs. George Fockler recited this prayer as published. It was also known to Dan Carey of Mt. Pleasant, James Stanley of Farwell, and Cripe Bailey of Harrison.

Blue Monday.
Bitter Tuesday.
Long Wednesday.
Everlasting Thursday.
Friday, will you ever go?
Sweet silver Saturday in the afternoon.
Sunday, may you last forever.
    Amen.
Two nights in the straw
And three meals ahead.

THE ROAD-ICER

To lessen the friction on the roads or even to build roads when snows did not come, some warm-dressed man or boy drove the sprinkler wagon during the cold nights. The job was not the most pleasant one in the lumber camps, but it needed to be done.

There is a legendary poet from the Tahquamenon country who supposedly is the author of a tribute to the "man who iced the roads." The author is said to have been an educated man who lived the life of a hermit in a shack between Newberry and Dollarville. Only these four lines of his tribute have I heard. They were given me by E. R. Crawford of Lake Orion.

There are some of us, I guess,
　　Call ourselves self-made men and such;
But then there was that other cuss
　　Went out and iced the road for us.

CHAPTER III

TRAGEDIES

OF THE

WOODS

Six whistles: six again — the fatal call
Which makes each man within the sound of it
Wipe the sweat from his eyes and, with strange chill
    at heart,
Ask, "What poor devil's got it now?"

Mrs. Rona Morris Workman of West Fir, Oregon, wrote this verse which portends tragedies in the woods. These tragedies frequently occurred at the log jams. James Loomis of Hobart wrote:

But before you try the powder
    Or to break her with the juice,
       Hand some peavies to the river rats and jacks.
They will roll her and they'll crowd her
    And they'll break the timber loose.
       Yes, they'll break her or a half a hundred backs.

One of those jam tragedies is the basis for the best-known song in the Michigan lumber camps, *The Jam on Gerry's Rocks* or *Foreman Jack Monroe*. It is known from Portland to Portland, and the famous rock or rocks can be found in almost any lumbering state.

Frank E. Lefler of Toledo, Ohio, insists that he has "talked with the men who helped haul the timbers to build the Garrish Dam on the Tittabawassee and who saw the names engraved on the hemlock tree below where the dam was built."

John Fitzmaurice in *The Shanty Boy* calls the foreman Charley Monroe and the girl Allie Farnum; he locates the tragedy on the Au Gres River.

The "maid from Saginaw town" is, depending on the singer, Allie Farnum, Clara Vernon, Clara Burnham, Clara Dennison, Clara Benson, or Clara Vincent. The version here came from Mrs. Dan McConnell of Rosebush, Liland Smock of Grayling, and Bill McBride.

THE JAM ON GERRY'S ROCKS

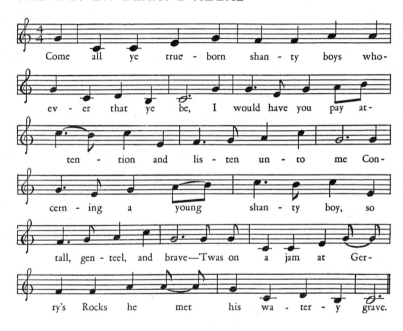

Come all ye true-born shan-ty boys who-ev-er that ye be, I would have you pay at-ten-tion and lis-ten un-to me Con-cern-ing a young shan-ty boy, so tall, gen-teel, and brave—'Twas on a jam at Ger-ry's Rocks he met his wa-ter-y grave.

1   Come all ye true-born shanty boys whoever that ye be,
I would have you pay attention and listen unto me
Concerning a young shanty boy, so tall, genteel, and
        brave—
'Twas on a jam at Gerry's Rocks he met his watery
        grave.

2   It was on a Sunday morning as you will quickly hear;
Our logs were piled up mountain-high, we could not
        keep them clear.
Our boss he cried, "Turn out, brave boys; your hearts
        are void of fear.
We'll break the jam on Gerry's Rocks and for Eagles-
        town we'll steer."

3   Now some of them were willing, but others hid from
        sight,
For to work on jams on Sunday they did not think it
        right.
But six of our Canadian boys did volunteer to go
And break the jam on Gerry's Rocks for their foreman,
        young Monroe.

4   They had not rolled off many logs till Monroe to them
      did say,
"I'd have you boys be on your guard; that jam will
      soon give way."
Scarce the warning had been spoken when the jam did
      break and go,
And it carried off those six brave youths and their fore-
      man, young Monroe.

5   When the rest of the shanty boys these sad tidings
      came to hear,
To search for their dead bodies to the river they did
      steer.
Some of the mangled bodies a-floating down did go,
While crushed and bleeding on the bank was that of
      young Monroe.

6   They took him from the water and smoothed down his
      raven hair.
There was one fair form among them whose sad cries
      rent the air;
There was one fair form among them, a maid from
      Saginaw town,
Whose sighs and cries would rend the skies for her
      lover that was drowned.

7 Fair Clara was a noble girl, the riverman's true friend;
  She with her widowed mother dear lived by the river's
   bend.
  The wages of her own true love the boss to her did pay,
  And the shanty boys for her made up a generous purse
   next day.

8 They buried him quite decently; 'twas on the first of
   May.
  Come all of you bold shanty boys and for your com-
   rade pray.
  Engraved upon a hemlock tree that by the grave did
   grow
  Was the name and date of the sad, sad fate of the
   shanty boy Monroe.

9 Miss Clara did not long survive her great misery and
   grief.
  In less than three months afterwards death came to her
   relief;
  In less than three months afterwards she was called to
   go,
  And her last request was granted: to be laid by young
   Monroe.

10 Come all of ye bold shanty boys who would like to go
and see
Those little mounds by the river's side where stands
the hemlock tree.
The shanty boys cut the woods all round; the lovers
there lie low;
Here lies Miss Clara Vernon and her true love, Jack
Monroe.

THE DEATH OF HARRY BRADFORD

1 Come all ye true-born lumbering boys, both fellows
young and old,
A story I will tell to you that'll make your blood run
cold,
Concerning a poor unfortunate lad who was known
both far and near.
He was killed on the deck at Essex Mill, as you will
quickly hear.

2 He walked out in the morning with little fear or doubt
That before the whistle blew at noon his life would be
crushed out.

The Jam on Gerry's Rocks was so well known that both parodies and serious imitations were to be expected. Some camp poet might have versified the drowning of Billy Barrelton at Snowtown Piers on the Muskegon River, for the superstition grew that Snowtown claimed a victim a year. Or he might have produced a ballad about Will Green who went down the long chute at Newaygo in July, 1887, to permanent injury.

Harry Bradford's tragedy was made part of the folklore literature by W. J. Taylor, a "camp poet." Harry was known to the Hockin boys; George Hockin of Kewadin witnessed the happening. The tragedy occurred at Phelps's camp north of Torch Lake.

E. J. Hollenbeck of Kewadin could not recall the complete ballad, but Edward Sayer of Cadillac had this version.

His father was the foreman here of this brave lumbering crew,
And he never dreamed that his son so dear would meet his fatal doom.

3 'Twas on the twenty-ninth of January in nineteen hundred two;
Little did we think a life'd be lost in our brave lumbering crew.
Little did we think in the morning that before the close of day
Our noble friend would be doomed to go to his cold and silent grave.

4 It is only three months ago since his little sister died.
Poor Harry was killed in this rollway; he'll be buried by her side.
On the thirty-first of January Young Harry was laid to rest.
His body was laid in the silent tomb; his spirit is with the blest.

5 And now I'll try to explain to you the last words that he said.

They chained the log and they set their hooks as they
    stood side by side.
He spoke up to his partner, saying, "I'll bet you a cigar
That this is the highest rollway that stands in this big
    yard."

6   "I'll bet you once," said his partner George, "there's
    another just as high."
"All right, we'll shake and make a bet," Young Harry
    he did cry.
He gave a waving signal to the lad that pulled the
    chain;
The team was quickly on the move, and he never
    spoke again.

7   The log came rolling up the skids, dropped over on the
    deck.
Every man was leaning on his hook, not a man of them
    did speak.
While the team was trying to jump the log, they scarce-
    ly made the raise;
The log dropped back and jarred the face, which sent
    him to his grave.

8   While the logs were rolling towards him, he tried to
        climb the tiers;
    To the very top of this highest deck Young Harry tried
        to steer.
    While trying to climb a large log, another one caught
        his hand,
    Which carried him back down in the jam as you will
        understand.

9   The logs came pounding over him like thunder from
        the skies.
    The boys they stood and gasped for breath when they
        saw that he must die.
    "Poor Harry's killed," Smith Rogers cried. "Come
        quick. Bring the team around.
    These logs must all be cleared away. His body must be
        found."

10   The chain was placed around the logs; they were
        quickly pulled away,
    So the boys could see down in the jam where the
        mangled body lay.
    His ribs were broke, his back was broke, his legs were
        broke also;

And his brains they lay beneath the deck in the cold
and bloody snow.

11   His father was on the road to camp when the dreadful
deed was done.
As soon as he reached the shanty, he heard news of
his son.
One of our crew spoke up and said, "Our rollway has
given way,
And an accident has happened. I have something
bad to say.

12   "Come down by the shanty—" And he slowly walked
away.
As they were walking down the road this young man
to him did say,
"Do you know that, Mr. Bradford, your Harry, he is
killed?"
"Oh no! I can't believe it, and I know I never will!"

13   And by the time they'd reached the jam where the
mangled body lay,
He walked up there within three rods and then slowly
turned away.

He walked back and forth with head bowed down with
    not a word to say,
While the boys were working fast to take his dead
    body away.

14   The dreadful news was carried to his kind old mother
        dear.
    No one knows how she must have felt when the sad
        news reached her ear.
    Little no one knows what dreadful pain has touched
        that mother's heart
    When the truth at last it came to pass that from him
        she must part.

15   I'll bid farewell to our noble friend that we will see
        no more.
    God bless his loving parents whose hearts will suffer
        sore;
    God bless his loving sister who'll mourn so silently;
    And now we'll say farewell, dear friend. He's gone to
        Eternity.

Marquette, Manistique, Menominee, Munising, Escanaba handled plenty of round stuff, but Seney was the Upper Peninsula town with the colorful reputation. In the days when Seney was "tough," Stub-Foot O'Donnell and Pump-Handle Joe met all trains and stood newcomers on their heads to shake out their pocket coins. Stuttering Jim Gallegher left hobnail marks on the faces of those who smiled at his affliction. Big Jim Keene was the "fightenest fool." Snap-Jaw Small bit off the heads of frogs and snakes for drinks. Notorious Silver Jack came to this town after being pardoned by Governor Luce. Jimmy Hale worked among such men.

Harry Evans collected this poem from Jack Hawkins of L'Anse who had been a creature of the forests since he was fourteen; the woods had been Jack's schoolhouse. Jack might have been called illiterate by some people, but if they'd ever been lost in the woods and been helped out by Jack,

SHANTY BOY'S ILL FATE

1   Gather round to me, you lumberjacks,
       And listen to my tale.
    I'll tell you of a shanty boy
       Whose name was Jimmy Hale.

2   He started out one autumn
       His fortune for to find;
    His mother tried to keep him home,
       But little did he mind.

3   He came upon our lumber camp
       And asked the 'push' for board.
    When he asked if he could swing an axe,
       He said he'd try darned hard.

4   They filled him up on flapjacks,
       Made his bed upon the floor.
    They told him he should hit the hay,
       That he'd be called at four.

they'd have found that there's lots of knowledge that doesn't involve reading or writing.

The "push" is a localism for foreman. A "widow-maker" is a long limb on a tree. Nearby lumberjacks have been known to miscalculate where the limb would hit when the tree fell. The name for the widow-maker was not facetiously coined.

5 I'm here to tell you shanty boys
      That kid sure knew his stuff.
He quickly learned to fell a tree
      And gave them room enough.

6 But one cold wintry morning
      As Jim worked hard by,
A widow-maker caught the lad
      And snuffed his young life out.

7 They took his body home again,
      All crushed and bruised so sore,
And placed it in his mother's care,
      Her live young boy no more.

8 Poor Mrs. Hale wept bitterly,
      But it did her no good;
Another shanty boy had met
      His ill fate in the woods.

JIMMIE WHALEN

Jimmie Whalen has carried a variety of names: James Whaland, James Wayland, James Phelan, George Whalen, and George Wayland. His story is well known, for it was collected by Franz Rickaby and by Carl Sandburg. I have heard it in the Great Lakes and Northwest timberlands. Tom Dunn of Gladwin stated that the incident occurred about 1882 during the drive on the Matawaski River, which the Canadians call the Mississippi.

James Priest of Flint, George Millard of Hillman, Perry Allen of Shepherd, Margaret Little of Rosebush, "Cherry Lane" Skinner of Weidman, and Bill McBride of Isabella City knew a version much like that in Carl Sandburg's *American Songbag*. Mrs. Frank LaNore and Miss Dorothy Dill from the Grand Traverse begin the ballad with "Come all ye tender Christians."

Nels Plude and Tom Dunn, two Garrish Dam lumberjacks, use these words.

1 Oh, it's come all you men and maidens wherever you
    may be,
   I'd have you pay attention and listen unto me.
 It is of one brave and bold young man; Jimmie Whalen
    he was called.
 He was drowned on McClaren's raft just below the upper
    falls.

2 Oh, the river ran with force and rage, the water was
    so high.
 Our foreman says to Whalen, "This jam you've got to
    try.
 You're young, you're strong and active. While danger's
    lurking near,
 You are the one to help us now to keep the water clear."

3 This brave, undaunted Whalen said unto his comrades
    bold,
 "Come one and all together, we'll do as we are told.
 We'll obey our foreman's orders, as noble men should do."
 Just as he spoke the dam it broke and let poor Whalen
    through.

4 The raging waters tossed and tore around from shore
  to shore.
 Now here, now there, his body went a-tumbling o'er
  and o'er.
One fearful cry for mercy, "O Lord, look down on me!"
His soul got free from earthly care, gone to eternity.

5 So come all you men and maidens a warning take from
  me.
 I hope you've paid attention and listened unto me.
Death will lurk around you; it's ready to destroy
The pride of many a father's heart, and many a mother's
 joy.

JIMMIE WHALEN'S GIRL

Franz Rickaby seems to have first recorded the story of Jimmie Whalen's girl. He picked up a three-stanza fragment from Will Daugherty of Charlevoix. Complete versions can be heard from Henry Babcock

1 Onward I strayed by the banks of a river,
  Viewing the sunbeams as evening drew nigh.
 As onward I rambled, I spied a fair maiden
  Weeping and wailing with many a sigh.

who ran the Pine River, Bill McBride, the Chippewa, Tom Dunn, the Cedar, Tom Hockaday, the Molasses, and Frank Cummins who ran the Tobacco. Tom Dunn sang six stanzas with a chorus.

Chorus

Weeping for that one that is now lying lonely,
　　Weeping for one that no earthly one could save,
For the dark rolling waters went madly around him,
　　And the grass now grows green over poor Jimmie's grave.

2　"Jimmie," she cried, "won't you come to my arms?"
　　　"Jimmie," she cried, "won't you come from your grave?"
"You promised this evening to meet me, my darling;
　　But Death's cruel angels have stole you away."

3　Slowly there rose from the depths of the water
　　　A vision of beauty as bright as the sun.
Bows of sweet crimson, they shone bright around them,
　　And to this fair maiden to speak he begun.

4　"Why have you called me from realms of glory
　　　Back to this world I soon had to leave?
To see you again I've come to you, darling;
　　I came back to you from my cold silent grave.

5 "Cold was the fight in the cold Mississippi;
   The water encircled me on every side.
 Thinking of you I encountered it bravely,
   Hoping in vain that you'd be my bride."

6 "Oh, Jimmie," she cried, "won't you linger here with
   me?
   Do not desert me in grief for to rave.
 Take me, oh, take me, along with you, darling.
   I'll lie down beside you in your cold silent grave."

HARRY BAHEL

The shingle-mill song about the death of Harry Bahel (Bail) can be definitely located in Lapeer County, Michigan, though it has been sung in Washington, Oregon, and Northern California. The year of the accident was 1879, the month, April, the day was the twenty-ninth. The names used are Harry Bail, Dale, Vail, Bell, and Hale; the correct name is Bahel.

1 Come all kind friends and parents,
   Come brothers, sisters, all.
 A story I will tell to you
   That will make your blood run cold.
 Concerning a poor, unfortunate lad
   That was known both far and near.
 His parents reared him tenderly
   Not many miles from here.

Grace Bahel Pregitzer of Onaway said that "three orphaned brothers, Mart, Charley, and Harry Bahel, worked their way from Chester, Pennsylvania, to Michigan's lumber woods in the 1870's. Harry was a lad of nineteen when he met his death in Arcadia Township in Lapeer County. This song was composed by brother Charley."

Frank Hatherly of Lapeer also said that the song was composed by Charley. However, another source said it was written by Harry's dearest friend, Johnny Coffee, who was later killed by a falling tree in the Georgian Bay country. Grace Bahel Pregitzer thinks that the song got into the Northwest through Mart Bahel, who "went west in 1880 and was never heard from afterwards." Many old-timers know the song. This is what Mrs. Pregitzer thinks is the "truest version."

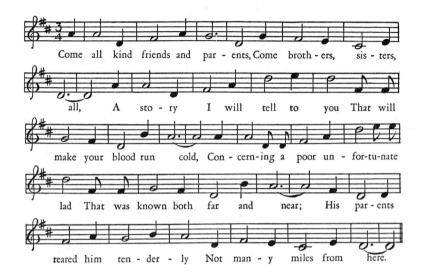

Come all kind friends and parents, Come brothers, sisters, all, A story I will tell to you That will make your blood run cold, Concerning a poor unfortunate lad That was known both far and near; His parents reared him tenderly Not many miles from here.

2 In the township of Arcadia
  In the county of Lapeer
There stood a little shingle mill;
  It had run about a year.
That's where this fatal deed was done
  That caused many to weep and wail.
That's where this young man lost his life;
  His name was Harry Bahel.

3 On the twenty-ninth of April
  In eighteen seventy-nine,
He went to work as usual;
  No fear on his mind,
Till the lowering of the feed bar
  Threw the carriage into gear
And flung poor Harry against the saw
  And cut him most severe.

4 It sawed him round the shoulder blade
  And halfway down the back.
It threw him out upon the floor
  As the carriage it came back.
He started for the shanty,
  But his strength was failing fast.
Said he, "My boys, I'm wounded bad,
  And I fear this is my last.

5 They sent for his dear brothers,
  Likewise his sisters too.
The doctor came and dressed the wound,
  But, alas, it was too true.

When his cruel wounds were dressed,
 He unto them did say,
"I know there is no help for me;
 I soon shall pass away."

6 No father had poor Harry
  To weep beside his bed,
No kind and loving mother
  To soothe his aching head.
He lingered for a day and night
  Till death did ease his pain.
Hushed are his words forever;
  He'll never speak again.

7 They dressed him for his coffin;
  They fitted him for his grave.
His brothers and his sisters
  Mourned the loss of a brother brave.
They took him to the churchyard,
  Where they laid him down to rest.
His body lies a-moldering there,
  And his spirit is with the blest.

DOWN BY THE WILD MUSTARD RIVER

There is white water in *The Wild Mustard River*. The ballad sings well if the voice is robust. The strapping young bull of the woods Walter Jordan of Nellsville first sang me this song; his mother recorded the music.

Locating the Wild Mustard River is no easy job. Floyd Darnell of Millbrook has said it is not Wild Mustard at all but Omuska. Marguerite Gahagan, who does a splendid job editing the *North Woods Call* in Johannesburg, has printed some interesting anecdotes about Kneeland, Bigelow, and Hansen camps but does not mention a Wild Mustard River. Alf Bauer of Hillman thinks the river flows out of McCormick Lake.

The first version came from Frederick Larke of Rogers City.

1   We were camped on the Wild Mustard River,
        Down by the Old Hendrick Dam.
    One morning as we rose from our blankets,
        We saw on the rocks a bad jam.

2   When the water comes rustling and rolling,
        Our pikes and peaveys we'd apply,
    Not thinking that one of our number
        That day had so horribly to die.

3   On round stuff there was none any better
        On the stream than our friend, Johnny Stile.
    He rode it more often than any
        And he always was reckless and wild.

4   But today his luck went against him,
        And his foot it got caught in the jam;
    And you know how that creek runs a-howling
        When we flood from the reservoir dam.

5   But we were all there in a moment,
        Just as soon as we heard his first shout,

For we knew that the waters were dangerous;
    They roll in but they never roll out.

6   We worked for an hour and a quarter
        Till our time it had come to a spare.
    We had got a big hole worked right through her
        When like lightning she hauled out of there.

7   When at length we reached the dead water,
        We worked till the sweat down us poured.
    We pulled his dead body from in under,
        But it looked like our Johnny no more.

8   Every bone in his body was broken.
        His flesh hung in shreds and in strings.
    We buried him down by the river
        Where the lark and the whippoorwill sings.

The second verson came from Walter Jordan of Nellsville and Roy Ellico of L'Anse.

1   Down by the Wild Mustard River,
        Down by the old Emric Dam,
    We arose from our blankets one morning
        To flood from the reservoir dam.

Down by the Wild Mus - tard Riv - er, Down by the old Em - ric Dam, We a - rose from our blan - kets one morn - ing To flood from the res - er - voir dam.

2 When the water came rustling and rolling,
   Our pikes and peaveys we'd apply,
 Not thinking that one of our number
   That day had so horribly to die.

3 On the river there was none any better
   On a log than my friend Johnny Styles.
 He had worked oftener than any other,
   And he always was reckless and wild.

4 But today his luck went against him,
   And his foot it got caught in the jam.
 And you know how that creek runs a-howling
   When we flood from the reservoir dam.

5 We rode her down to dead water
   And worked till the sweat down us poured.
 We pulled his poor corpse from in under
   But it looked like our Johnny no more.

6 His flesh was all cut up in ringlets
   And rolled out as flat as your hand.
 There'll be peace on this earth for his body
   While the Lord holds his soul in command.

LES REEDER

A rollway as defined by Fred Burke of Marinette, Wisconsin, is "an inclined way on the river ice or bank down which logs being unloaded from sleighs were rolled and piled up." Rollways and jams have provided considerable material for the folk singers. Here is one from the skidways.

This accident happened about eight miles northeast of Lake City, which was once called Reeder and where members of the Reeder family still reside. Calvin Thomas of Jennings, Walter Jordan of Nellsville, and Lester Howe of Houghton Lake knew this verse.

1 Now you've all heard of the pinewoods boys,
    And how some of them died.
But have you heard of Les Reeder's death
    And how his loved ones cried?

2 'Twas on the twenty-third of September
    In the year of 'ninety-four.
And Les's mother had begged of him
    To work Sundays no more.

3 But Les put on his coat and cap
    And started for the door,
Saying it would be his last work,
    He'd work Sundays no more.

4 Bill Shrader, he worked up above,
    And Les worked down below.
They were sending big logs up the skids
    As big logs ought to go.

5   'Twas the first log on the second tier—
        They did not think 'twould stay.
    But Shrader thought it was safe enough
        So he's not to blame you see.

6   And Les stepped in between the skids.
        "Look—" was all Shrader said.
    And as Les looked up and smiled
        The big log struck his head.

7   Then Shrader jumped down from above;
        He did not lose his head.
    They rolled the big log off from Les,
        But, alas, poor Les was dead.

8   They took him back to his brother's house,
        Where ended his last sad rites.
    But his awful death will haunt their dreams
        Through many lonely nights.

9   Now you've read of rich men's deaths,
        How some of them have died,
    But you couldn't say half enough for Les,
        No matter how you tried.

TEN LITTLE WORDS

A. B. Belcher of Toledo, Ohio, a conductor on the Ann Arbor Railroad, said that these quatrains came from the woods.

1   Ten little words was all it said.
          It's on their way they hum.
     "Kiss Mother for me," it singing says,
          "For I'm too poor to come."

2   And each one gave him freely
          From out of his scanty store,
     For him to see his dying mother.
          Her son would see once more.

3   Ten little words was all it said.
          It's on their way they hum.
     "Kiss Mother for me," it singing says,
          "For I'm too poor to come."

HARRY DUNN

The story of Harry Dunn (or Dunne) probably crossed from Canada to Michigan and then traveled westward. "The county of Odun" may be "the country of Aldouaine" in New Brunswick, for Canadian bluenoses

1   I once did know a fair young man,
          His name was Harry Dunn.
     His father was a farmer
          In the county of Odun.

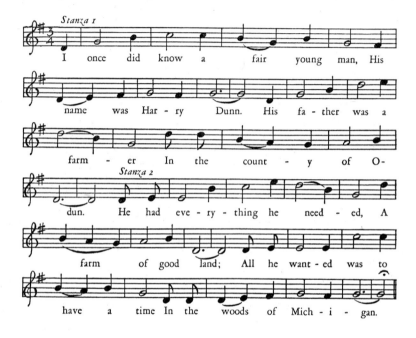

knew the verses. A version from Peter Glade, Micmac Indian guide and logger of Pubnico, Nova Scotia, is printed in *Lore of the Lumber Camps.* It is also known to a Micmac lumberjack of my acquaintance, Hank Peters of Truro, Nova Scotia.

In Michigan the shanty boys mention either Pinconning or St. Helen, both of which are north of Bay City.

2   He had everything he needed,
    A farm of good land;
All he wanted was to have a time
    In the woods of Michigan.

3 The morning Harry left his home
   His mother to him did say,
 "Oh, Harry dear, take my advice
   And do not go away.

4 "Don't leave your aging parents,
   Likewise your sisters three;
 There is something tells me
   No more your face I'll see."

5 But Harry only laughed at her,
   Saying, "Mother, do not fear,
 For winter will soon be over.
   In springtime I'll be here

6 "With lots of money for you to spend.
   And don't you understand
 That I only want to have a time
   In the woods of Michigan?"

7 Harry started for Bay City,
   Hired to a lumbering crew.
 The next place that he found himself
   Was the woods of Pinconning.

8 He worked along for three months,
   And ofttimes he'd write home,
 Saying, "Winter will soon be over
   And in springtime I'll be home."

9 One morning Harry rose from his bed;
   On his face he wore no smile.
 He called his comrade outside the door
   Whose name was Charlie Tile,

10 Saying, "Charlie, I had a dreadful dream,
   Which fills my heart with woe;
 There is something seems to tell me
   It's home I ought to go."

11 But Charlie only laughed at him,
   Which pleased him for a time.
 Then Harry said to Charlie,
   " 'Tis time we'd fell a pine."

12 They worked along till ten o'clock
   All on that fatal day,
 Till a falling limb came down on him
   And killed him where he lay.

13   His comrades circled around him
        And dragged the limb away.
    I was standing right beside him,
        These words I heard him say,

14   "Oh, come right now. I'm dying;
        My hour will soon be near.
    May the Lord in his good mercy
        Look upon my parents dear."

15   In two or three days after that
        His coffin was sent home,
    Containing all that was left on earth
        Of poor, poor Harry Dunn.

16   And when his mother saw him,
        She fell down like a stone.
    They picked her up but her heart was broke
        When Harry he came home.

17   Likewise his poor old father
        Was never seen to smile again;
    And two or three months after that
        They buried the poor old man.

18   Come all of you true lumbering boys,
        Wherever you may be,
I'd have you pay attention
        And listen unto me.

19   Don't leave your aging parents;
        Stay at home if you can;
And if you're forced to leave your home,
        Stay away from Michigan.

GROUCHY BILL

This story of the Brule hero was rhymed by Arthur M. Quirt of Iron River. It was published in the *Menominee Herald-Leader* (1943).

1   Yes, I know Bill was grouchy,
I know he was sometimes tough;
Still to me, the way I see,
He had p'ints what was good enough.
I know he was no ways social
And never had no pal,
But he spent his money like the rest of us,
And was busted spring and fall.

2   I remember the spring he went under,
I can't just say what year;

He was running jam for Jimmy Doyle,
I was with Golden on the rear.
We had just sluiced through the Carney,
The Wheeler Dam was full,
When word came up to the rear crew,
There was a jam on the "Little Bull."

3   We all hiked down next morning
Though our feet were skinned and sore.
We had our lunch at Saunders,
Reached the tail of the jam at four.
Of course we had to wait for water.
We got a good night's rest.
Give ten hours in the hay to a river hog
And you bet he thinks he's blessed.

4   We let the water off at the Wheeler,
Lifted the gates of the Carney at seven.
The push, he said he thought the head
Would hit the jam at eleven;
And such a bunch of river hogs,
A hundred men or more,
Each with a peavey in his hand,
Lined up along the shore.

5   I'd say we had high water;
The jam was twelve logs high.
In the rear, the banks were overflowed;
In the front, it was almost dry.
We picked, we horsed, and we blasted,
Used teams with block and line,
A better crew the work to do
Would be doggone hard to find.

6   We worked away to about three o'clock,
When we saw her commence to haul.
In the front, the water began to rise,
In the rear, it began to fall.
For a while she kept groaning and grinding,
Then broke with an awful roar.
Each man grasped his peavey tight
And beat it for the shore.

7   We all got safe but a farmer boy,
He came from near DePere;
There he was out on that whirling jam,
Just paralyzed with fear.
Loud above the din and roar
For help we heard him cry.

We heard Bill mutter to himself,
"I'll save that boy or die."

8   Out he jumped on the round stuff,
Sure-footed as a squirrel;
The log never grew could put him in,
No matter how fast she'd birl.

9   He was down and up, and up and down,
But kept on with a steady will.
One hundred men were watching him,
One hundred hearts stood still.
We saw him as he reached the boy.
We saw the logs up-end,
We saw them working toward the shore,
As they passed around the bend.

10   Yes, we found them two days after,
About two miles below,
So crushed and bruised that you'd wonder
Who they was if you didn't know.
When the Head Push runs the sieve
To pick out the good and true,
To my mind I think you'll find,
He'll be picked for the main river crew.

11 Yes, I know Bill was grouchy,
   I know he was sometimes tough;
   Still to me the way I see,
   He had p'ints what was good enough.

12 The old Brule River keeps rolling on,
   Flows o'er the "Little Bull";
   Her waters sing an idle song,
   There's no more jams to pull.

13 No more will the voice of the river hog
   Be heard on the morning air,
   No more will the cook at the wanigan,
   His morning meal prepare.
   No more will the bull cook say,
   "Take her boys, your hungry stomach fill."
   They all have gone. Yes, every one,
   To the home of Grouchy Bill.

In a land covered by pine trees it is not surprising that Pine rivers were too common to suit geographers. In Lower Michigan were two Pine rivers famed for lumber. One of these was in the famous Saginaw valley. The other rises in Wexford County, flows west of Tustin, turns northerly and flows west of Hoxeyville, and empties into the Manistee above High Bridge. *Jim Brooks* was composed in one of the camps of Louis Sands on the Pine River. It was remembered by Bird Williams of Tustin.

JIM BROOKS

1   What became of Jim Brooks, did you ask me?
     O stranger, I'm blamed if I know;
But I think he has hiked to some country
     Where there is no logs and no snow.

2   Although I can't tell you for certain,
     I believe that they took him away
Along with the angels in heaven
     At the close of one cold winter's day.

3   I don't think that God would be willing
     To go back on a fellow like Jim.
He was only a lumberjack, stranger;
     But no one was truer than him.

4   Although he was rough and unpolished,
     He never would stand for a bluff;
And when he hit town with his stake,
     He always cut loose like a tough.

5   "Hi, Jerry! Hi, Billy! Ye devils,
     Step up here and have one on me."

That's the way he would talk to his comrades,
    And his money went easy and free.

6   It was down on the Yellow Dog River
        We lumbered that winter and spring.
    The canthooks and peavies re-echoed
        And made all the forest to ring.

7   A log-hauler's wife did the cooking,
        And she certainly fed us good chuck.
    Such sausage and pancakes ain't common;
        We envied that log-hauler's luck.

8   She was blessed with a bright little youngster.
        A pretty and sweet-natured lad,
    Whose voice was the joy of the pinery,
        Whose laughs made the wilderness glad.

9   I confess that I once got a fancy
        That angels way up in the sky
    Were jealous to have him in heaven,
        So they dropped him on earth from on high.

10   One day the lad took a notion
        To watch how they brought down a tree,
  And ran right straight to the sawyers,
        All eager and anxious to see.

11   The proud and great giant pine tree
        Came toppling, and roared on its way.
  Jim Brooks met his death as he carried
        The child safe out of harm's way.

12   So I don't think God would be willing
        To go back on a fellow like Jim.
  He was only a lumberjack, stranger;
        But no one was truer than him.

CHANCE MC GEAR

The McGears lived at Williamsburg in Grand Traverse County. Like many a youth of his day the young Chance McGear wanted to spend a winter in the woods. Against parental advice he went into Kalkaska

1   Come all ye true-bred shanty boys,
        Come listen unto me,
  And likewise pay attention
        To hear what I have to say.

County and hired out to load for Smith and Blisby. The date of his accident, January 9, 1892, is correct according to John Fleming of Bellaire and Tom Jones of Manistee. This song, patterned after *Harry Dunn,* was given me by Floyd Darnell of Millbrook.

2   'Tis of a true and gallant youth
        Who's known both far and near;
His parents raised him tenderly;
        His name is Chance McGear.

3   His father did say unto the boy,
        While his heart with grief did swell,
"O son, I think you'd better stay at home,
        For I think you'll do as well."

4   But Chance, being young and active,
        He knew not trial nor strife;
He headed for the lumber woods
        To gain a start in life.

5   He started for Kalkaska,
        A place we all know here,
And then a job he soon secured
        About ten miles from there,

6   To load for Smith and Blisby,
        A firm we all know well.
But Heaven have mercy on him now,
        For he's gone to his happy home.

7 This being the ninth of January,
   In eighteen ninety-two,
He started out to load the cars,
   And with a jolly crew.

8 This being his day to top-load,
   The logs were all in place.
He mounted right up to the top
   With trouble at his face.

9 And in the loading of the car
   Was where the troubles all begin,
But little did he realize
   The troubles he was in.

10 His partner being bossinger
   He used the upper shelf;
He sent the logs up to the top,
   For 'twas his partner's will.

11 But Chance was young and active;
   He mounted, set the hotch.
The driver being cautious,
   He stopped again at the notch.

12 But the logs being very slippery,
   One end did swing around.
 The only chance the poor boy had
   Was jumping to the ground.

13 The poor boy he sprang backward
   And then was forward thrown.
 He struck down beside the car;
   Then came the fatal blow.

14 He lay up in the crossties,
   All too faint to raise his head.
 The first blow was supposed to be
   Enough to strike him dead.

15 His partner being active,
   He came to his relief
 And moved the logs from off him
   While his heart did swell with grief.

16 The blood was streaming from his mouth
   And likewise from his ear.
 Heaven have mercy on his soul
   Whose name was Chance McGear.

17 The company showed their respect;
   They cared for him quite well.
  They sent him down to Williamsburg,
   Where his parents they did dwell.

I have had no success locating the region where John Robertson and Joe McCarthy did their chopping. This is the Carl Lathrop—Frank Hufford version of the song.

JOHN ROBERTSON

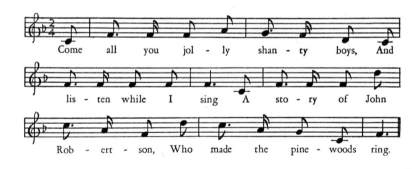

1 Come all you jolly shanty boys,
   And listen while I sing
  A story of John Robertson,
   Who made the pinewoods ring.

2 He was the best dang lumberjack
  That ever here was seen:
His coat was tore and dirty
  And he was never clean,

3 But underneath this ragged front
  He had a heart of gold;
He never feared a single thing.
  For he was brave and bold.

4 One night a greenhorn came to camp,
  He was too green to live;
He didn't know an awful lot;
  His head was like a sieve.

5 He'd come out from the city;
  His mother she was sick;
He 'lowed he'd earn some money
  So she'd get well right quick.

6 He never done a tap of work
  As all the boys could see,
And when he asked us for a job
  The boss he laughed with glee.

7   Said he, "My man, it's NO;
       You couldn't earn your keep."
The lad he sighed and turned away
       And looked about to weep.

8   John Robertson rose slowly up
       And to the foreman said,
"You better take him on, old man;
       I'll show him to his bed."

9   Next morning Joe McCarthy,
       For that's the greenhorn's name,
Was put to work at chopping,
       Which is no easy game.

10   The greenhorn worked with John
       At chopping of the pine.
With old John's help he soon became
       A lumberjack quite fine.

11   One day in late October
       He was working on a tree.
The tree was rotten in the core,
       But this he could not see.

12 He kept on chopping till too late;
   There was an awful crack.
 John Robertson he gave a yell;
   He cried, "Hey, Joe, stand back!"

13 But Joe was petrified with fear;
   He couldn't even move.
 Then John ran up behind him
   And gave him a hard shove.

14 They both fell flatly to the ground,
   And Joe he was thrown free.
 He laid there in a kind of daze;
   But John he couldn't see.

15 We raised the tree almighty quick.
   The boys were awed and hushed,
 For there we saw the form of John,
   Who lay quite torn and crushed.

16 He looked at Joe and said, "My boy,
   I know that I am through;
 On account of your dear mother
   I'm glad 'twas me, not you."

17 They buried him among the pine
   And wrote above his grave,
 "He gave his life beneath a tree
   Two others for to save."

18 This brave act that old John had done,
   It was not done in vain,
 For Joe's ma was restored to health
   And was made well again.

Only slightly less well known than the terrible Peshtigo Fire of Wisconsin and the Tillamook Blaze in Oregon is the fire of 1871 in the Thumb of Michigan. Though another terrifying forest fire devastated the area ten years later, when old-timers talk about "the fire" they mean the fire of 1871.

The fate of the McDonald family of Huron County is not unlike that of others in the Fire of '71. It was supposedly set to verse by Cyrus McTaggart of Bad Axe.

THE MC DONALD FAMILY

1 Sons of freedom, only ponder
   On McDonald's awful doom,
 And his family, five in number,
   In the hot and fiery gloom,

2 Where the flames in torrents flashing,
   Through the fields and forest round,
 And the trees like thunder crashing
   In great numbers on the ground.

3   Thus the deluge, fierce in motion,
        With the winds did loudly roar
Like the waves upon the ocean,
        Dashing on the stormy shore.

4   What have been their thoughts and feelings
        In that hot and dismal place,
When the flames came round unyielding,
        Such a stubborn foe to face?

5   Oh! methinks I see them weeping,
        Clasped within each other's arms,
When the flames came round them sweeping,
        Cry aloud in wild alarms.

6   As they cast their eyes to heaven
        And for mercy loudly cried
When by flames and smoke were driven,
        Where they fell and shrank and died.

7   Thus the deluge passed o'er them;
        Sad and awful was the scene,
Sweeping everything before them
        Through the wild and living green.

8   Thus it raved until the morrow;
        Then a calm appeared at last.
    Every soul was filled with sorrow
        At the closing of the blast.

9   All the fields and forest timber
        By their friends were searched around,
    And at length in death's cold slumber
        These poor souls' remains were found.

10   In the woods where they were driven
        Lay their bodies on the earth,
    And the souls we hope in heaven
        With the God who gave them birth.

11   All ye who listen, only ponder.
        Can you think without regret
    On the death of this small number
        And amongst them poor Jeanette?

12   A maiden fair in every feature
        And admired by all around
    As a lady and a teacher
        In this mouldering mass was found.

13   Those horrid flames so fierce, and raken
        By the wind with force and strife,
This fair lady they have taken
        In her prime and bloom of life.

14   No more she's seen among the flowers
        Nor in the shade of summer green
With her friends in idle hours.
        This fair maid no more is seen.

15   She is gone from earth, departed
        From her friends, to be no more,
Left them sad and broken-hearted
        To lament on Huron's shore.

16   May to her a robe be given.
        May her precious soul be blest
Like the stars in yonder heaven
        And be one among the rest.

Until iron hoops replaced wooden ones, the hoopmaker was important to forest products. The hoopmaking industry demanded straight-grained black ash trees, and the Great Lakes lumber woods had great quantities of it. Indians were superior workmen with ash; they handled the froe very well. The Indian has used black ash for making utensils since time immemorial.

William Thatcher of Grand Rapids, known to the Chippewas as Big Tooth, sings *The Dying Hoopmaker* to the tune of *Bingham on the Rhine.*

THE DYING HOOPMAKER

1   A hooper lay dying
        'Neath a sultry summer sky;
In the green depths of a black ash swamp
        He had laid him down to die.
His comrades clustered round him
        And the tears came rolling down,
As they tried to lift the heavy tree
        That pinned him to the ground.

2   The sweat rolled down their faces
        As they tried to ease the weight
That crushed their comrade's life away
        As merciless as fate.
The only sound that could be heard
        Through that tight-lipped, silent crew
Was the rasping shriek of the cross-cut saws
        As they cut the tree in two.

3   "It's no use, boys. I'm going home,"
        The dying hooper cried.
"I've courted Death for many a day,
        And now he's caught my stride.

I am passing on to the Great Beyond
    To a better land I know,
Where all good hoopmakers find a home
    When it's time for them to go.

4   "Draw nearer, partners, nearer.
        I'll tell you while I can,
I have an aged mother
    Way back in Michigan.
The tears stood in her dear old eyes
    As she begged me not to roam;
Her heart would break if she saw me now
    So many miles from home.

5   "Then there's my little sweetheart.
        I know she'd weep for me
If she saw me crushed and bleeding here
    Beneath this black ash tree.
She told me when I left her
    That I'd better stay at home,
But I was wild and wayward
    And I was bound to roam.

6   "My father was a hooper too.
          They say that I'm like him.
    Like me he died in harness,
          Pierced by a falling limb.
    In the swamps of Upper Michigan
          He died ten years ago.
    I let the rest take what they would,
          But I kept my father's froe.

7   "Please send it to my mother;
          She'll know from whence it came.
    And write to her a line or two
          And tell her I died game.
    Then dig my grave here in the swamp
          At the foot of some ash tree,
    Where the squirrels and chipmunks chatter
          And the birds sing merrily.

8   "Come close. I cannot see you
          In this swiftly fading light.
    A cloud has passed across the sun
          And hid it from my sight.
    I reckon I am going, boys;
          I'll bid you all good-bye.

It's getting darker, partners.
    Oh God! It's hard to die!"

9   A shudder shook the hooper's frame
        And wracked his tortured chest;
Then his head fell back among the leaves,
        And we knew that he'd gone West.
He died with a smile on his fair young face;
        And his bright wide-open eyes
Seemed trying to follow his spirit's flight
        To its home beyond the skies.

10   In the deep shade of the forest
        Where the ferns and flowers wave,
Where the wood thrush sings the sweetest
        Is a lonely moss-grown grave.
For we buried him under a black ash tree
        In the green depths of the swale
With these few words written above his head,
        "Here ends a hooper's trail."

CHAPTER IV

The lumberjack's unwritten code was that "no man could offend, insult, or molest a woman on the street; no man could speak lightly of a woman of good reputation without suffering swift and violent justice at the hands of his fellows," says J. E. Nelligan in his **Life of a Lumberman.** In my quarter-century of collecting folklore among the lumberjacks, the women of my household have met many woodsmen, but they have never heard any blasphemy or vulgarity from them. The lumberjack respects ladies. Yet any city "belle" who thinks she has found a sucker in a mackinaw is in for a surprise. I like to remember how two painted ladies were amazed at the shrewdness of three old lumberjacks in mackinaws down Broadway, when some of us were in New York. Those plaid shirts covered a clever technique, I observed.

THE LUMBERJACK AND HIS GIRLS

According to Paddy Miles of Big Rapids, the young, rough lumberjacks were controlled by rules at the camps, too. Said Paddy: "These men knew the rules. Here they are: no fighting on the river, no drinking on the river, and to bed at 9 o'clock."

182

THE FLAT RIVER GIRL

I'm a bro-ken - heart - ed rafts-man, from Green-ville I came. I court-ed a las - sie, a lass of great fame. But cruel - heart - ed Cu - pid has caused me much grief; My heart it's a - sun - der, I can ne'er find re - lief.

Flat River rises in Six Lakes, has a splendid mill-site at Greenville, and empties into the Grand River near Lowell. It is in what was a great pine belt of Michigan. A lively incident there is the basis of the song. When it was composed, Greenville was a small logging town and Anne Tucker's home was just across the street from her father's blacksmith shop. In the late 'sixties big, burly, red-haired Dan McGinnis came to town. Dan knew Jack Haggerty, a good-looking fellow from Hart and Shelby. Neither Dan nor Jack was permitted to keep company with pretty Anne Tucker. McGinnis, a clever entertainer as well as a good raftsman, was assigned to the camp where George Mercer, Anne's fiancé, had been promoted to woods boss. McGinnis was so aroused that he composed this shanty song, using Haggerty's name to conceal his own identity. At first Mercer was so angry that he would not permit the song sung in camp, and the Tuckers disliked it. In time the family aversion wore away, and Anne herself is said to have sung it to her Canadian friends.

1   I'm a broken-hearted raftsman, from Greenville I came.
I courted a lassie, a lass of great fame.
But cruel-hearted Cupid has caused me much grief;
My heart it's asunder, I can ne'er find relief.

The Flat River Girl may be the best known shanty boy ballad on the Lake Michigan slope. It is sung to several tunes, no one being quite sure what tune Dan McGinnis first used.

The words and tune of the first version came from Bill McBride.

2   My troubles I'll tell you without more delay,
A comely young lassie my heart stole away;
She was a blacksmith's only daughter from Flat River side,
And I always intended for to make her my bride.

3   I brought her rich jewels and the finest of lace;
With the costliest of muslins it was her I'd embrace.
I gave her my wages for her to keep safe;
I begrudged her nothing that I had myself.

4   My name is Jack Haggerty where the white waters flow;
My name it's engraved on the rocks of the shore.
I'm a boy that stands happy on a log in the streams.
My heart was with Hannah, for she haunted my dreams.

5   I went up the river some money to make;
I was steadfast and steady, I ne'er played the rake.
Through Hart and through Shelby I am very well known:
They call me Jack Haggerty, the pride of the town.

6 One day on the river a letter I received.
She said from her promises herself she'd relieved;
She'd be wed to a young man she'd a long time delayed,
And the next time I'd see her she would not be a maid.

7 Then adieu to Flat River. For me there's no rest:
I'll shoulder my peavey, and I'll go out West;
I'll go to Muskegon some pleasures to find,
And I'll leave my own Flat River darling behind.

8 So come all you jolly raftsmen with hearts stout and
   true,
Don't depend on a woman; you're sunk if you do.
And if you chance to see one with dark chestnut curls,
Just think of Jack Haggerty and his Flat River girl.

The second version came from Jake Fry
of Middleton.

1 I'm a broken-hearted raftsman, from Greenville I came.
My name is departed, the loss is my fame.
In shop and in household I am very well known:
They call me Jack Haggerty, the pride of the town.

2   I'll tell you my troubles without more delay,
How a sweet little lassie my heart stole away;
She was a blacksmith's daughter from the Flat River
      side;
I always intended to make her my bride.

3   Her form like the dove it was dainty and neat;
Her hair hung in ringlets to her pretty white feet.
She was a blacksmith's daughter from the Flat River
      side;
Her words were like music o'er the rise of the tide.

4   I dressed her in muslins and the finest of lace;
In the costliest of raiment her form I embraced.
I called her my jewel, what a gem for a wife!
When I think of her treachery, it near takes my life.

5   I know all the country where the Flat River rolls;
I know all its sand bars, its rocks, and its shoals.
I'm the boy that stands happy on the white rolling
      streams.
My thoughts were on Anna; she haunted my dreams.

6   I worked on the river; I earned quite a stake.
I was steadfast and steady; I played not the rake.
I gave her my wages, the same to keep safe;
I begrudged her nothing that I had on this earth.

7   One day on the river this letter I received:
She said from her promises herself she'd relieved
To wed with her true love, this long time delayed,
And the next time I saw her she would not be a maid.

8   To her mother, Jane Tucker, I lay all the blame;
She caused her to leave me and go back on my name;
She has broken the rigon that God would soon tie
And caused me to wander till the day that I die.

9   Farewell to Flat River. For me there's no rest.
I'll shoulder my peavey, and I will go west;
I'll go to Muskegon some comfort to find.
Farewell to Flat River and the gay girl behind.

10   Come all you old rivermen with hearts strong and true,
Don't depend on a woman; you are beat if you do.
If ever you see one with brown chestnut curls,
Just think of Jack Haggerty and the Flat River girl.

·The third version, both tune and words, is that sung by Carl Lathrop of Pleasant Valley, Sam Hackett of Wheeler, Harry Blackman of Breckenridge, and Henry Babcock of Alma.

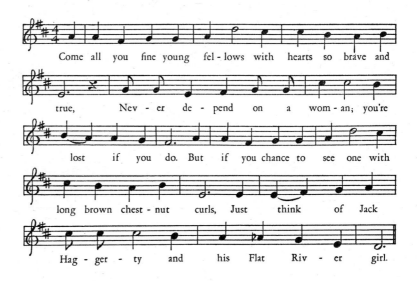

Come all you fine young fellows with hearts so brave and true, Never depend on a woman; you're lost if you do. But if you chance to see one with long brown chestnut curls, Just think of Jack Haggerty and his Flat River girl.

1   Come all you fine young fellows with hearts so brave
        and true,
    Never depend on a woman; you're lost if you do.
    But if you chance to see one with long brown chestnut
        curls,
    Just think of Jack Haggerty and his Flat River girl.

2   Her form was like the dove, so slender and so neat;
Her long brown chestnut curls hung to her tiny feet;
Her voice was like the music or murmurs of the breeze
As she whispered that she loved me as we strolled
      among the trees.

3   She was a blacksmith's daughter from the Flat River
      side,
And I always had intended for to make her my bride;
But one day on the river a letter I received
Saying that from her promise herself she had relieved.

4   To her mother, Jane Tucker, I lay all the blame;
She caused her to leave me and to blacken my name.
I counted her my darling, what a lady for a wife!—
When I think of her treachery it nearly takes my life.

5   Come all you fine young fellows with hearts so brave
      and true;
Never depend on a woman; you're lost if you do.
But if you chance to see one with long brown chestnut
      curls,
Just think of Jack Haggerty and his Flat River girl.

Tom B. Jones of Manistee, timber cruiser at 78, took a crew from the Canfield Mill in Manistee to California. From Tom came this version of *Bung Yer Eye*, which appears in S. E. White's *Blazed Trail*. This version from the Lake Michigan slope was also known to George Andrews of Arcadia, Fred Hirzell of Moorestown, and Andy Alguire of Baldwin; no two of them agreed on the identity of Long Tom who "bossed the whole shebang." K. G. Kueken of Howard City was certain that Big Dan who "played the fiddle" was either Dan McArthur or Dan McGilbert. Kueken recalled that "I asked Dan's brother, Gib, once what his name was. He said sometimes its was Gilbert McArthur and sometimes Arthur McGilbert."

BUNG YER EYE

1   I love a girl in Manistee;
        She lives with her mother.
I defy all Michigan
        To find such another.
She's tall and slim, her hair is red,
        Her face is plump and pretty.
She's my daisy, Sunday-best-day girl,
        And her front name stands for Kitty.

Chorus
    Bung yer eye! Bung yer eye!

2   I took her to a dance one night;
        A sailor did the bidding.
Long Tom bossed the whole shebang,
        And Big Dan played the fiddle.
We danced and sang the livelong night,
        With fights between the dancing,
Till Long Tom cleaned out the whole damn place
        And sent the sailors prancing.

Chorus
    Bung yer eye! Bung yer eye!

The second version came from the Lake Huron slope. It was known to E. K. Hardenburg of Saginaw, Everett Smith of Edgewood, Henry S. Babcock of Alma, James Gilfoy of Bay City, and Dan Carey of Mt. Pleasant. Dan Carey said that Silver Jack and Big Dan were more notorious along the Saginaw than were Broken-nose Kelly and Roaring McLeod along the Muskegon and the Manistee.

1   I love a girl in Saginaw;
        She lives with her mother.
I defy all Michigan
        To find me such another.
She's tall and slim, her hair is red,
        Her face is plump and pretty.
She's my daisy, Sunday-best-day girl,
        And her front name it is Kitty.

Chorus
    Bung yer eye! Bung yer eye!

2   I took her to a dance one night;
        A mossback gave the bidding.
Silver Jack bossed the shebang,
        And Big Dan played the fiddle.
We danced and sang the livelong night,
        With fights between the dancing,
Till Silver Jack cleaned out the place
        And sent the mossbacks prancing.

Chorus
    Bung yer eye! Bung yer eye!

THE CURST WIFE

The records show that many sons of the British Isles sawed and chopped in the woods. These woodsmen may have been the ones who knew the old ballads and gave them new words. An interesting example is the woods version of Child 605. Though this version from the sprightly Britisher Thomas E. Webster is good, it is not as interesting as the one I picked up in the Ozarks in Arkansas just south of the Missouri line.

1   The old Devil he came to a woodsman one day.
Said he, "One of your family I would take away."
Ti-rum-ti-diddle-dum-dido.

2   "Oh," said the woodsman, "I'm all undone.
For I hate to lose my oldest son."
Ti-rum-ti-diddle-dum-dido.

3   "It's not your oldest son I crave,
But your scolding wife I'm bound to have."
Ti-rum-ti-diddle-dum-dido.

4   "Oh, take her and welcome with all my heart.
I hope you two never more will part."
Ti-rum-ti-diddle-dum-dido.

5   The Devil he took her upon his back
And off to Hell went clickty-clack.
Ti-rum-ti-diddle-dum-dido.

6   One little devil cried out in his pains;
She picked up a club and knocked out his brains.
Ti-rum-ti-diddle-dum-dido.

7 Another little devil climbed up on the wall,
  Saying, "Take her back, Daddy, she'll murder us all."
   Ti-rum-ti-diddle-dum-dido.

8 Another little devil jumped into the well,
  Saying, "Take her away, Dad, she'll ruin all Hell."
   Ti-rum-ti-diddle-dum-dido.

9 So the Devil he roped her up in a sack
  And off to the woodsman he carried her back.
   Ti-rum-ti-diddle-dum-dido.

10 The woodsman he laughed, for it tickled him well
  For to think that his wife was the bully of Hell.
   Ti-rum-ti-diddle-dum-dido.

THE SHANTY BOY AND THE MOSSBACK

Gardner and Chickering in *Ballads and Songs of Southern Michigan* have a song entitled *The Mossback*, which the authors say came from Pennsylvania. This rhymed narrative or argument was not unlike *The Big Eau Claire* from Wisconsin. Paul Bunyan Criss, well-known West Virginia axeman, sang the song, and Glen Meek of Vancouver, Washington, can speak it for the Northwest. So, it seems, this piece is quite well known among the timber cutters.

Criss sang of "Saginaw town"; "Pete" Petersen of Sand Lake sang of "Hinton town"; these words and this tune are largely from Benjamin Needham of Flint, Carl Gullekson of Cadillac, and Pete Petersen.

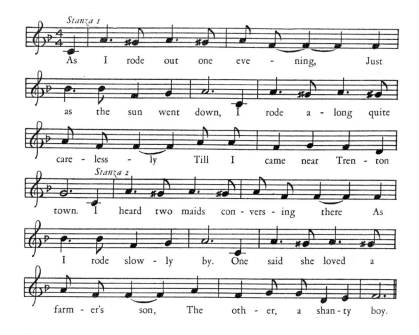

1   As I rode out one evening,
        Just as the sun went down,
    I rode along quite carelessly
        Till I came near Trenton town.

2   I heard two maids conversing there
      As I rode slowly by.
   One said she loved a farmer's son,
      The other, a shanty boy.

3   The one that loved a farmer's son,
      These words I heard her say:
   The reason why she loved him was
      Because with her he'd stay.

4   He would stay with her all winter;
      To the woods he would not go;
   And when the spring it comes again
      His ground he'd plow and sow.

5   "Oh! how you praise your farmer's son,"
      The other one did say.
   "If his crops should prove a failure
      His debts he could not pay.

6   "If his crops should prove a failure
      Or the market get too low
   The sheriff then would sell him out
      To pay the debts he'd owe."

7   "As for the sheriff selling out,
      You need not be alarmed;
  For there's no use of being in debt
      When you are on a farm.

8   "On a farm you earn your bread
      Without working in snow and rain,
  While the shanty boy works hard each day
      His family to maintain."

9   "Oh! how I love my shanty boy,
      Who goes off in the fall.
  He is both stout and hearty;
      He's fit to stand the squall.

10   "With pleasure I'll receive him
      In the spring when he comes down.
  His money he will spend quite free
      While you mossbacks have got none."

11   "Oh! how you praise your shanty boy,
      Who to the woods must go.
  He's ordered out before daylight
      To work in storms of snow.

12 "While happy and contented
   With my mossback I will lie,
 And he'll tell me tales of love
   While the storms they pass us by."

13 "Oh! I cannot stand that soft, soft talk,
   Those mossbacks' sons do say;
 For some of them they are so green
   The cows'd eat them for hay.

14 " 'Tis easy for to know them
   When they come into town,
 For the small boys all do gather round
   Saying, 'Mossy, hoe 'er down.' "

15 "Of what I've said of your shanty boy
   I hope you'll pardon me,
 And from that ignorant mossback
   I'll try and get me free.

16 "And if ever I get a chance
   With a shanty boy I'll go.
 I will leave that mossback
   His ground to plow and sow.

17 "So here's health to Dodge and Co.,
    Those enterprising men,
Who for the good of Michigan
    Are doing all they can.

18 "And here's health to the shanty boy,
    Who makes the wildwoods ring.
They fall their pine in the wintertime
    And drive them in the spring."

ON THE BANKS OF THE PAMANAW

One of the better lyrics sung by the lumberjacks of the Great Lakes is *On the Banks of the Pamanaw*. The tune is reminiscent of the Irish ballad, *Dream of a Fair Maid*. When O. A. Webster of Millersburg sang the song, he called the stream "Pemanaw"; Bill McBride and Pat Battle and Ernie Losey called it "Pamanaw." Mrs. William Garchow of Farwell called it "Panama." Fred Bush and I tramped down the Chippewa River one snowy March day looking

1 While strolling out one evening,
    In the latter part of June,
The sun had sunk far in the west,
    And brightly shone the moon.

2 I strolled away from camp, my boys,
    To view the scenery round;
'Twas there I spied this Indian maid
    A-sitting on the ground.

for the grizzled lumberjack Bill McBride, who, nearing 80, was snaking deadheads out of the river. He sang us the song on the windward side of a corn shock; Bush took down the music while I got the words.

Where the song originated is not known for certain. The Menominee basin seems to have the soundest claims. The Wisconsin Pembine, though, could easily be called Pamanaw by some singing jack. Up in the Arrowhead country of Minnesota it was suggested that the song came from across the state at Pembina. In my search for its source, I went over to the Red River of North Dakota, south of Winnipeg, but found no one who knew the song. Of course, that fact means only that no one was found who knew it, and nothing more. The lumberjacks have long since left that area.

3 As I advanced up towards her
  She did not seem afraid;
I boldly stepped up to her
  And unto her I said,

4 "You do surprise me very much,
  Although you're but a squaw,
To see you here so lonely on
  The banks of the Pamanaw."

5 "Draw nigh to me, young man," she says,
  "And I will tell you all,
The truth I will unfold to you
  And the cause of my downfall.

6 "My brother and my sister died,
  Likewise my pa and ma;
They left me here so lonely on
  The banks of the Pamanaw.

7 "And that's not all, young man," she says,
  "A lover once was mine.
He was a true, bold Indian scout
  On the British bounty line.

While stroll - ing out one e - ve -

ning, In the lat - ter part of

June, The sun had

sunk far in the west, And

bright - ly shone the moon.

8   "He courted me and he flattered me,
　　　　Called me his lovely squaw,
　　But now he's gone and left me on
　　　　The banks of the Pamanaw."

9   Says I, "My pretty, fair maiden,
　　　　Come go along with me.
　　I'll take you to a better land,
　　　　To a paleface counteree.

10   "I'll dress you up in costly robes,
　　　　The likes you never saw.
　　No more you need to ramble on
　　　　The banks of the Pamanaw."

11   "Oh, no! Oh, no! young man," she says,
　　　　"And this you may very well know,
　　For I have given, oh, my oath
　　　　To live with the red deer and doe.

12   "For the white man may break his oath,
　　　　And though I'm but a squaw,
　　I'll live and die and keep my vow
　　　　On the banks of the Pamanaw."

THE LITTLE EAU PLEINE

It seems that *The Little Eau Pleine* is the best-known lumberjack song from Wisconsin. It was known by many Michigan jacks, for there were many hardy sawyers and choppers and rivermen who worked in both Michigan and Wisconsin camps.

This song was written by W. N. Allen of Eau Claire. Some Michigan jacks have the name wrong, since they knew neither French nor Wisconsin: Bill McBride, Perry Allen, Ottis Turpenning, George Hockin, and Alvin Royce sang of "the little low plain."

One eve-ning last June as I ram-bled The green woods and val-leys a-mong, The mos-qui-to's notes were me-lo-dious, And so was the whip-poor-will's song. The frogs in the marsh-es were croak-ing, The tree toads were whis-tling for rain, The par-tridg-es round me were drum-ming, On the banks of the Lit-tle Eau Pleine.

1 One evening last June as I rambled
   The green woods and valleys among,
 The mosquito's notes were melodious,
   And so was the whippoorwill's song.
 The frogs in the marshes were croaking,
   The tree toads were whistling for rain,
 The partridges round me were drumming,
   On the banks of the Little Eau Pleine.

2 The sun in the west was declining
   And tingeing the treetops with red;
 My wandering feet bore me onward,
   Not caring whither they led.
 I happened to see a young schoolma'am;
   She mourned in a sorrowful strain;
 She mourned for a jolly young raftsman
   On the banks of the Little Eau Pleine.

3 I stepped up beside this young schoolma'am,
   And thus unto her I did say,
 "Why is it you're mourning so sadly
   When all nature is smiling and gay?"
 She said, "It is for a young raftsman
   For whom I so sadly complain.

He has left me alone here to wander
    On the banks of the Little Eau Pleine."

4   She said, "Alas, my dear Johnny has left me.
        I'm afraid I shall see him no more.
He's down on the lower Wisconsin;
        He's pulling a fifty-foot oar.
He went off on a fleet with Ross Gamble
        And has left me in sorrow and pain;
For 'tis over two months since he started
        From the banks of the Little Eau Pleine."

5   "Will you please tell me what kind of clothing
        Your jolly young raftsman did wear?
For I also belong on the river
        And perhaps I have seen him somewhere.
If to me you will plainly describe him
        And tell me your young raftsman's name,
Perhaps I can tell you the reason
        He's not back to the Little Eau Pleine."

6   "His pants were made out of two meal sacks,
        With a patch a foot square on each knee.

His shirt and his jacket were dyed with
    The bark of the butternut tree.
He wore a large open-faced ticker,
    With almost a yard of steel chain,
When he went away with Ross Gamble
    From the banks of the Little Eau Pleine.

7   "He wore a red sash round his middle,
    With an end hanging down at each side.
His shoes, number ten, were of cowhide,
    With heels about four inches wide.
His name was Honest John Murphy,
    And on it there ne'er was a stain;
And he was as jolly a raftsman
    As was e'er on the Little Eau Pleine.

8   "He was stout and broad-shouldered and manly,
    His height was about six foot one;
His hair was inclined to be sandy,
    And his whiskers as red as the sun.
His age was somewhere about thirty.
    He neither was foolish nor vain.
He loved the bold Wisconsin River
    Was the reason he left the Eau Pleine."

9   "If John Murphy's the name of your raftsman
        I used to know him very well.
But sad is the tale I must tell you:
        Johnny was drowned in the Dell.
They buried him 'neath a scrub Norway;
        You will never behold him again;
No stone marks the spot where your raftsman
        Sleeps far from the Little Eau Pleine."

10   When the schoolma'am heard this information
        She fainted and fell as if dead.
I scooped up a hatful of water
        And poured it on top of her head.
She opened her eyes and looked wildly,
        As if she was nearly insane,
And I was afraid she would perish
        On the banks of the Little Eau Pleine.

11   "My curses attend you, Wisconsin!
        May your rapids and falls cease to roar!
May every low head and sand bar
        Be as dry as a log schoolhouse floor!

May the willows upon all your islands
    Lie down like a field of ripe grain
For taking my jolly young raftsman
    Away from the Little Eau Pleine.

12   "My curse light upon you, Ross Gamble,
    For taking my Johnny away!
I hope that the ague will seize you
    And shake you down into clay!
May your lumber go down to the bottom
    And never rise to the surface again!
You had no business taking Johnny Murphy
    Away from the Little Eau Pleine.

13   "Now I will desert my vocation;
    I won't teach district school any more.
I will go to some place where I'll never
    Hear the squeak of a fifty-foot oar;
I will go to some far foreign country,
    To England, to France, or to Spain,
But I'll never forget Johnny Murphy
    Nor the banks of the Little Eau Pleine."

THE BIG EAU CLAIRE

The lumberjacks in the region of the Great Lakes usually traveled around, getting work in more than one state. It is not surprising, then, that a Wisconsin song is known by Michigan lumberjacks. The city of Eau Claire in Wisconsin is a colorful city of woods memories.

This production came to me from Charles Petersen of Morley.

1   Come all you jolly lumberjacks
        And listen to my song.
It's one I've just invented;
        It's one that's ten years long.
It's of a brisk, young damsel,
        So gallant, young and fair,
Who dearly loved a shanty boy
        Upon the Big Eau Claire.

2   The shanty boy was handsome;
        There was none more gay than he.
In the summertime he labored
        In a mill at Mosinee;
But when winter came along
        With its cold and wintry breeze,
He worked upon the Big Eau Claire
        Cutting down the big pine trees.

3   He wore a heavy black moustache,
        A head of curly hair;
A fairer boy than he was not

Upon the Big Eau Claire.
He loved the milliner's daughter.
He loved her long and well,
But circumstances happened
The which I hate to tell.

4 The milliner said, "A shanty boy
My daughter shall not wed."
But Sally didn't give a darn
For what her mother said.
She packed up her waterfalls
And bonnets by the stack
And started another milliner's shop
'Way down at Fond du Lac.

5 Now she is broken-hearted
And wearied of her life.
She dearly loved the shanty boy
And wished to be his wife.
So when bonny boy came along
A-reaping of his crops,
She went down to Baraboo
And went to picking hops.

6   It was in this occupation
       She found but little joy,
For thoughts came rolling o'er her mind
       About the shanty boy.
She took the scarlet fever,
       Laid sick a week or two.
It was in the Colby prison house
       At the town of Baraboo.

7 Sometimes in her raving
   She tore her amber hair
And talked about the shanty boy
   Upon the Big Eau Claire.
The doctors tried but all in vain;
   Her life they could not save.
And now the yellow willows
   Are drooping o'er her grave.

8 When the shanty boy heard of the news,
   He became a lunatic.
He acted just as others do
   When they become lovesick.
He hid his saw in a hollow log
   And traded off his axe,
And started as a captain's boy
   On the fleets of Sailor Jack.

9 He fell into the rapids at
   The falls of Mosinee,
Which brought an end to his dear life
   And all his misery.
The old Wisconsin River
   Is sweeping o'er his brow.

His friends and his relations
    Are weeping for him now.

10   The milliner is bankrupt;
        Her shop is going to wreck.
Sometimes she thinks of moving
        Away from Fond du Lac.
Her pillow's haunted every night;
        It is by her daughter fair
And the ghost of the shanty boy
        Upon the Big Eau Claire.

11   So, all of you fair maidens,
        Take advice from me.
Don't be too quick to fall in love
        With every boy you see,
For shanty boys are rowdy
        As everybody knows.
They dwell up in the pinewoods
        Where the mighty pine tree grows.

12   A-stealing logs or shingles,
        Or a-telling of big lies,
A-playing cards at evening,
        Is all their exercise.
But if you want to marry
        For comfort and for joy,
I'll advise you to get married
        To some honest farmer boy.

BEBE HUNG ONE ON US

E. J. Petersen, known to his friends as Pete Petersen, is a talented lumberjack. Pete had always wanted to write, so when he gave up the canthook and axe, he took up the pen. His *North of Saginaw Bay* sold well and pleased many, and his *White Squaw* did nearly as well. Pete gave me this one.

1   I am a jolly shanty boy,
        My age is seventeen.
I am the biggest sucker,
        I'll bet you've ever seen.

2   Now, I could start to lay the blame,
        But 'twould be better said,
Just to say I've got a brother
        And my brother's name is Ed.

3   Now, Eddie had a girl
         And her name was Bebe Sack.
    He asked her if she'd marry him;
         She said it was a whack.

4   But she said, "My dear Eddie,
         Before we're joined for life,
    You should have a little cabin
         For to keep your little wife."

5   He says, "My dear Bebe,
         For your own sweet sake,
    I'll go up in the lumber woods
         And try to raise a stake."

6   And she says, "My dear Eddie,
         You are the man to win.
    Here's a kiss to bind the bargain."
         And she hove a dozen in.

7   Now, I didn't have a chance to win,
         Not a thing to gain.
    But I came up to the lumber woods
         With Eddie, just the same.

8   We worked both late and early;
        We toiled through rain and snow,
    And sent our checks to Bebe,
        Who was saving up the dough.

9   Then one day there came a letter;
        It was from Bebe's brother Fred.
    And if it wasn't the dangest news
        That man has ever read.

10   We sat down to read it,
        And this is what it said:
    Bebe had married a butcher,
        And the butcher's hair was red.

11   We read a little farther,
        And you'd ought to hear us swear;
    For Bebe had a baby
        And the baby had red hair.

12   What they'd done with all our dough
        The letter never said,
    But Bebe hung one on us,
        And were our faces red.

MONIKER SONGS

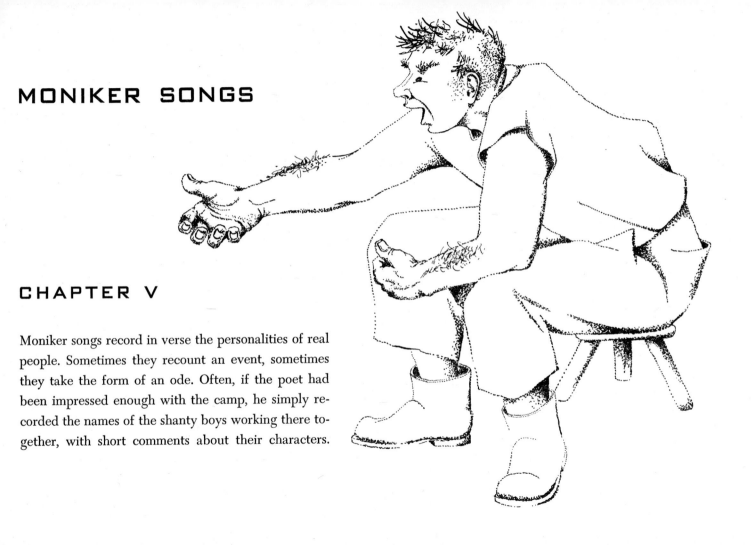

CHAPTER V

Moniker songs record in verse the personalities of real people. Sometimes they recount an event, sometimes they take the form of an ode. Often, if the poet had been impressed enough with the camp, he simply recorded the names of the shanty boys working there together, with short comments about their characters.

The timberlands had numerous logging railroads, many of which were narrow gauge. They have long been abandoned; trees a foot in diameter are growing on the rights-of-way. One of these logging railroads — the Boyne City, Gaylord, and Alpena — is mentioned in *Timekeeper's Lament*.

Gus A. Benson of Cadillac supplied these words.

TIMEKEEPER'S LAMENT

1 Come railroad men and comrades, come hear my tale
of woe.
It's of some hustling work we done, not many years
ago.
It was on the B. C., G., and A., a railroad of renown,
To get the people o'er the state and cut the timber
down.

2 Art Franks, the first man on my list, stood just six foot
and eight,
He cussed his men severely if they were a minute late.
"Come, boys, jump on the lining bars, act lively, don't
be slow.
If you jump to my music, I will never let you go."

3 Our little bald-headed foreman was on the job each
day.
He was as cool as an iceberg, and he surely made it
pay.
The section men along the line to his commands
jumped quick,
Because his first name started Ira and his last wound
up with Crick.

4   L. H., our superintendent, alias Peter Clutch,
Came growling Monday morning, but we didn't mind
    him much.
"Good morning, lads. How are you? What makes you
    feel so blue?
Come jump into the rigon; we've got lots of work to
    do."

5   The grade was made, the ties were laid, and steel
    came in its turn.
To reach the town of Atlanta, our hearts did daily
    yearn.
O'er hills, through swamps and valleys, we wound our
    weary way.
We heeded not the snow and rain; so they caused no
    delay.

6   On the fourteenth of October, in the year 1914,
Our hearts were all aflutter, each eye shone like a
    bean.
We reached our destination, twenty minutes of nine,
We drank to success of the railroad. God bless us, we
    felt fine.

7 And now since our work is ended, we can go our lonely
  way
And think of the ups and downs we had on the B. C.,
  G., and A.
I can hear the rumble of the train as it clatters o'er
  the rail.
I know our work has been okayed; so once more I hit
  the trail.

PADDY HART

W. B. Laughead, California lumberman, from Westwood, Lassen County, is responsible for *Paddy Hart*. He wrote this paragraph which he sent me along with the copy: "This version was sung by Sam Eastman, who left Saginaw for California headed by Dick Hovey, and Eastman wrote this version from memory for Hovey, who sent me a copy. Eastman said this song was

1 Come all you gallus sporting men and boys that fall the
  pine,
I hope you'll pay attention and just listen to this rhyme.
In this piece of composition from the truth I'll ne'er
  depart
In the praises of that lumberman they call young
  Paddy Hart.

composed by one Big Head McGinness, who also wrote 'White River Drive.' As I recall this song, it had a stanza about each of the characters, including Paddy Hart." The stanza he remembers is as follows:

There's Big Head McGinness, he's next in our song;
And to tell you his pedigree won't take me long.
He says he is Scotch, but I think he's from Cork;
And he'd rather drink whisky than do honest work.

2　Paddy sprang from a line of kings named Brian Fitz-Gerald O'Lane,
Who fought in the time of Brian Boru and from Ireland drove the Dane.
On his mother's side was a soldier bold by the name of Kefe McGlone,
Who lived in a castle made of mud in the bogs of sweet Tyrone.

3　Paddy's social education his parents did neglect,
But he was schooled in the art of self-defense near the suburbs of Quebec.
The latter place we now know well was Paddy's native town,
Where he started first upon the turf that gave him such renown.

4　Paddy's fighting weight was seven stone ten; his height was five foot six.
He could whip his weight in wildcats, and numerous were his tricks.
There's Burns, McGraw, and Muffraw, three men of well-known skill,
Fell victims to his cunning art, and he made them cry their fill.

5 He was full of wit and humor, and a card among the
   boys.
 With a bottle of whisky at his side he'd turn grief into
   joys.
 He was true to friend and square to foe, no matter
   when or where;
 Meet poor Paddy where you would, you'd find him on
   the square.

6 But there's one thing carried the boy away: 'twas
   his love for women and wine.
 He was the pet of the fancy wherever he went; he was
   dressed both gay and fine.
 There was a widow lived close by, and the dogs stared
   on her path;
 He used to take her out to ride in his father's old
   calash.

7 So one night Paddy started out full bent upon a lark.
 He struck a chum, another rough, and they started
   after dark.
 A gallon of whisky Paddy took; Lame Bob, a case of
   beer.
 And they started for Kate Phillips's, her lonely heart
   to cheer.

8 When they got there, 'twas getting late; the widow had
   locked her door.
 Who wouldn't pity Paddy's fate? Half froze he'd yelp
   and roar:
 "Get up, me darling. Let me in, or I shall surely freeze.
 Some presents, ma'am, I've got here. I know they will
   you please."

9 "Go 'way from here, you drunken bum," the widow
   then did say.
 "What will become of my good name if you come here
   this way?
 The neighbors they will see you. I'm sure they are not
   blind.
 So pick up your tracks and leave this place; no lodging
   here you'll find."

10 Then Paddy cursed and swore God dam', and he drank
   a whole bottle of gin,
 Kicked in the door, and with the jug split her face from
   nose to chin.
 She called for Wallace, the eldest son, to fetch her the
   old shotgun
 And blazed away slapbang at his head with buckshot
   number one.

11 Then Paddy keeled over in the snow, and for help he
   loud did cry.
 His gallant chum took to his heels and left Paddy there
   to die.
 He lay all night in the cold snow; no gentle hand was
   near
 To soothe the breast of Paddy Hart or give the poor
   boy cheer.

12 At length some woodsmen passed that way, and at-
   tracted by his groans
 They carried him home on a big pine slab, and the
   doctor cured his wounds.
 And by careful nursing he got well and healthy by
   degrees,
 But he never since was known to fight or go off on such
   sprees.

13 And now he's quit his drinking, and he's living on the
   square;
 And for respectability none with him can compare.
 His sporting life he's given o'er, and you must understand
 He's married and gone out West, where he tills a piece
   of land.

14 So all you gallus sporting men, of reckless life beware.
Some future day, be it late and before old age on you
stare,
Some old widow in her wrath, when good feelings all
depart,
Will draw upon your carcass as she did bold Paddy
Hart.

'WAY DOWN NEAR ALPENA

Scotty McDonald of Alpena remembered the song which was collected as a fragment by Franz Rickaby.

1 'Way down near Alpena in a far-distant land
There is a hard-hearted, hard-spoken band
Called paythens, gorillas. They don't use much care
And they're hard to manage when they get on a tear.

Chorus

Hurray, hurrah! For the fruit you can bet.
Let's take a drink, boys, for our credit's good yet.

2 It was just the other night they got on a tear
Sam Gluffin vowed he could whip any man there.
Charlie Kittson climbed him as he lay on the sod,
But Sam Gluffin fears nothing on the footstool of God.

3   The other night in Jim Woodrickson's Saloon
Jim Todrick whipped Donnell, who thought himself
    some.
Sam Gluffin brought home a gallon to wind up the
    spree,
Saying, "This is the kind of hairpin I be."

4   "Whiskey, dear whiskey, from the hour of my birth
Is dearer to me than what else on earth.
For days I have labored and days have I toiled
And many a dollar for you have I spoiled."

OUR FOREMAN, MR. KNIGHT

This versified remembrance of one of Thunder Bay's foremen, a woods boss from the roaring lumber days, was furnished by Max Wolter of Hillman. Mr. Wolter lives down in the Black River country.

1   Mr. Knight is our foreman's name;
    A good old soul is he.
He works us from morning till night
    On potatoes, salt, and tea.
      But that's all right,
      It's Mr. Knight.

2   Why should we worry and fret?
       He turns us in on rainy days
After we are all wet.
       Our shanty is a dandy hall.
Our bunks are where
       The bedbugs feed and deermice stall.

3   Our vegetables are bulleys,
       Red horse beans and bread.
Our waiter is a pretty maid,
       And she has never wed.

4   Here we are good lumberjacks
       Working day and night.
We never will forget this job
       And our foreman, Mr. Knight.

Lumberjacks had numerous rollicking songs about their work. Some songs were sung far and wide, carried from camp to camp as the men moved. Other songs with a strong local flavor originated in camps and grew in length as some versifier added new stanzas to fit camp happenings. Matt Deschaine of Menominee recalls *Camp Seven Song* from his days at Pete Arseneau's Camp on Pine River.

CAMP SEVEN SONG

1   It was early in October, fall of 1896,
    I found myself in Menominee and in an awful fix.
    We hired out to Arseneau the timber to cut down.
    Two million feet must be complete before we reach the town.

Chorus
    Run, Mack! Jump, Jim! Be careful what you do
    To make the timber clatter, for Arseneau will put you thru.
    Hired out to Arseneau the timber to cut down.
    Two million feet must be complete before we reach the town.

2   Here's to Mr. Arseneau. I'll tell you he's right there.
    It keeps him pretty busy to drive the old gray mare.
    And when his day's work is done, and he sits down to rest,
    He's wishing for some mossback girl to lean upon his breast.

3   Here's to our dandy cookee, I'll have you all to know.
    And see him slash the hasher-box; dishes down they go.

Oh, the boys are getting plumpy, as fat as any duck;
Their clothes will hardly fit them 'cause they get such
    bully chuck.

4   Here's to the loaders, the top sleighs to load.
They stand right near the skidways, all on the icy road.
With peavey bars and hand spikes, oh, merrily they
    fly.
Just keep the logs a-booming, boys. We'll catch them
    on the fly.

5   Here's to Camp Seven. It is the heart's delight.
To curse and damn each other and sometimes have a
    fight.
With peavey bars and hand spikes, oh, merrily they fly.
You better keep away from them unless you want to
    die.

6   Here's to Mr. Hatfield and Mr. Sanders too.
There goes Dan McAllister and all his dandy crew.
And when we get to Menominee we'll see those girls
    so fine.
We'll forget about those stormy days we worked upon
    the Pine.

Jut Gannon is far from good verse; it is about as halting as *Budd Lake Plains*. Seldom does a collector get such crude verse; time has a way of engulfing the worst of this homemade "poetry."

Thomas G. O'Donnell of Flushing, Long Island, has stated that he knew Jut Gannon in 1884. The O'Donnells were then lumbering Greendale and dumping their logs in the Chippewa River. Jut worked in various capacities in the woods.

Jule Corlew of Gladwin (mentioned in the song), the Reetz brothers of Rose City, Floyd Armstrong (the "old Professor") of Gladwin, and Marvin Norton of Lake City knew certain characters named.

Mr. and Mrs. Howard Malcomnson of Beaverton furnished the words and music.

JUT GANNON

1   Ed Coan says, "Jut Gannon, I want you to drive team."
Says Jut, "By the Jesus, I'll drive them by steam."
So early next morning Jut Gannon arose,
And off for old Nolan he did go.

Chorus
Lily-ding-ding, ding-lily-ding

2 He put on his load with a devil of a show;
   Before he got out he called for a tow.
   The way he cussed it was a sin,
   But the cussing didn't keep him from sinking in.

3 Along came Jule Corlew all happy and stout;
   Says he, "Jule, I'll be here all night if you don't
     pull me out."
   Now Jule being small and his team being strong,
   Two lifts and a pull, and it did not take long.

4 There was Roy Major, who drives the black mules,
   And they are only a pair of tough fools.
   He hitches on a log and he tells them to go;
   Old Jack shakes his head as if he says no.

5 There was Frank Lambert, who drives the red bulls;
   And, O Lord Jesus, how they can pull:
   He hitches on a log and tells them to go,
   And he is the boy who don't need a tow.

6 There was old Hank Eddyburn, a big bag of wind;
   He'll make you a canthook that hangs on a limb.

So early next morning when you go out for the hook,
Says Hank, "By the Jesus, I know you were stuck."

7   There was Carl Major, you all know him well;
He goes to old Nolan, gets drunker than hell;
He comes home next morning neither dead nor alive
And swears to the boys that he ain't got a louse.

8   So it's all day Sunday he'll sit in his bunk
With all his shirts off, and his lice he will hunt.

OLD DAVID WARD

David E. Ward was born in Keene, New York, September 15, 1822. He came to Newport (Marine City), Michigan, in 1836. He married Charlotte Rust and then persuaded Amasa Rust to come to Michigan from Wells, Vermont. Amasa was the

1   Come all you young fellows,
      I'll sing you a song;
It's my own invention,
      And I won't keep you long.

father of the five Rust boys of Saginaw, who later operated in Wisconsin, Minnesota, Ontario, Washington, Oregon, California, and Florida. John Rust opened a lumber outlet in Cleveland. Amasa and Ezra were famous on the Saginaw. Aloney and David were almost as famous in Eau Claire, Wisconsin.

In 1851 David Ward received his medical degree from the University of Michigan, though he seems never to have had a patient except himself. In 1851 he "explored" the Tittabawassee, Pine, and Chippewa rivers. In 1852 he explored the "pine lands at the headwaters of the Cass," Chippewa, and Big Salt. In 1853 he "looked over" cork pine along the White River north of Muskegon for Charles Merrill. In May he "traveled up to Houghton Lake by pony trail from the mouth of the Tobacco River." That fall he "selected ten lots of cork pine" on the Upper Peninsula Pine River, which "was eventually sold for $55,000 to Arthur Hill of Saginaw."

In 1860 he lumbered two jobs on the Chippewa, "one where Mt. Pleasant now is and the other three miles below Midland." In 1877 he started lumbering the Manistee.

2   'Twas a bright morning
      I started away,
And off to the woods
      I expected to stay.
I packed up my turkey
      When I found a good pard,
And we both went a-lumbering
      For old David Ward.

Chorus
Sing fol-de-diddle-di-roo
Ri-doodle-di-day.

3   And now I will tell you
      The style of our camp:
If the boys didn't kneel down
      They were sent off to tramp;
There was many a good man
      Who got his discharge,
For they kept small boys there
      Who were not very large.

The ghost town of Deward on the upper Manistee is an old D. E. Ward camp. From 1885 to 1893 he purchased 70,000 acres of hardwood in northeast Michigan. The reader will find David Ward's autobiography an interesting record of lumbering and lumbermen.

The version of *Old David Ward* here published, I believe came from Isaac Fancher.

4   Now there was the foreman,
         A very nice man;
     He was always at work
         And contriving some plan.
     Your pockets he'd pick,
         And your clothes he would sell,
     And get drunk with the money
         At the Greening Hotel.

5   And there was old David
         Along with the rest,
     Like an old setting hen
         Just come off from her nest.
     He'd click and he'd clack
         And he'd look rather blue,
     And he'd swear at the boys
         Who went soldiering through.

6   And there was a scaler,
         I almost forgot;
     He was the worst ratapat
         In the whole bloomin' lot.
     If he was sent off
         To get his just dues,

> He'd go to heaven barefoot,
>> Without any shoes.

7   And now to conclude
>> And to finish my rhyme,
> For to sing any more
>> I don't feel inclined.
> I'm out of the woods
>> And won't be back again
> To be turned out long hours
>> In the snow and the rain.

THE EAST JORDAN LINE

The lumberjack talks about women more often than does the cowhand, perhaps; but the jack has much less to say about women than some writers indicate. John Gargett of Alma has a Duck-foot Sue who is "long-waisted in the feet," also remembered by Clair Stauffer of Vestaburg.

1   I came to Gladwin on September the tenth;
> I went to Fred Rutley's and my money I spent.
> I picked up a paper and there I did find
> a "WANTED GOOD MEN" on the East Jordan
>> Line.

Chorus
> Lack-fol-de-de-daro, lack-tul-dru-le-a.

A few "poems" like *East Jordan Line* mention the "girls" with no great respect. In fact, there are more "bunkhouse" versions of this one than there are "parlor" versions. Tom Dunn of Gladwin and Jack Fathey of Midland could recite the rollicking versions. Alf Levely of Edenville, Parks Allen of Ithaca, and Sam Veyette of Grand Marais had more printable ones.

2   Here's to myself; I have no loud squeals.
I'm having a snap; I'm on the big wheels.
The spokes are of wood and the rims are of steel.
I wish Bob Hegersoll had them to eat in a deal.

3   Here's to our blacksmith; you all know him well.
He's burned more iron than's on this side of hell.
The son of a bastard, he's burned up more coal.
And his tongues are much worse than a crooked elmpole.

4   Here's to one of our teamsters; he thinks he is some.
My opinion of him: he's a son of a gun.
He skids with the tongue; he can't use a dray;
And he can fool around longer than the pole of a sleigh.

5   We'll come down to Gladwin some day in the spring.
The whistles will blow and two bells will ring.
Bill McSweeney will play and Red Balby will call,
And we'll have a big dance in the Gladwin town hall.

6   Oh, the pretty wee girls are numerous around here.
    You can tell by their eyes that they're fond of their
        beer.
    They will come to a dance and they'll whorl round and
        round.
    But there ain't a good girl in the whole bloomin' town.

JUST TO MAKE A CHANGE IN BUSINESS

Bill Hart, a prominent lumberman who died at Jack's Spur in the Upper Peninsula, cut timber one winter on Turtle Lake. The mess crew of that camp was a colorful lot, long remembered by the Turtle Lake shanty boys. The cook, equally noted for her avoirdupois and doughnuts, owned a bicycle, which she bounced over the tote roads at some risk to the vehicle. The cookee was an attractive miss named Lillie Clark. They have been immortalized in this song, the words of which were secured by Mrs. Gladys Covington and the music by Mrs. Alma Seel.

1   Since new things are all the rage
    In this great and glorious age,
        On a few things I will surely propound.
    It's of things I'd like to see
    And of things that ought to be
        Just to make a change in business all around.

2   Now our cook she's got a bike,
    And she takes it down the pike,
        And many a double-header she takes on the
        ground.

236

Since new things are all the rage In this great and glo-rious age, On a few things I will sure-ly pro-pound. It's of things I'd like to see, And of things that ought to be, Just to make a change in busi-ness all a-round.

If she'd buy a little book
And just study how to cook,
> What a change it'd make in business all around!

3 Now, I'll sing of Lillie Clark:
She's a beauty after dark.
> And for mashing men she can't be downed.

But to catch a farmer guy
She must wink the other eye
> Just to make a change in business all around.

4 Now I'll sing about the push
Who goes singing 'round the bush;
> But a better man to watch for can't be found.

But if his wife ever catches on,
There will be a different song;
> And 'twill make a change in business all around.

5 Now my song it is composed,
And to danger I'm exposed;
> But I think I have the lumberjacks all down.

But to make the thing look fair,
We'll build castles in the air
> Just to make a change in business all around.

CHAPTER VI

BUNKHOUSE

BALLADS

The ballad collector follows many false trails before he meets a Bill McBride; in fact, he may never meet one. I can remember many false trails in twenty-five years of collecting. The summer of 1938 I spent twelve happy days in the blueberry country of the Upper Peninsula following a hot trail from Strongs to Paradise to Grand Marais, but without getting a single ballad. Another summer I roughed it for a fortnight among pulpwood cutters from International Falls, Minnesota, to Kenora, Ontario, without publishable results. In 1946, a week in the Minnesota Paul Bunyan country from Brainerd to Bemidji produced nothing much. The next year three of us got as far as Flin Flon, Manitoba, and ended with three fairly good mining ballads. In 1952 very little came out of the Wyoming tie camps and Montana and Idaho lumber camps. In 1955 a week on Sugar Island produced nothing new, and two weeks along Lake Superior very little. But there is always a chance of meeting a Marion Ellsworth, an Ottis Turpenning, a Perry Allen, a Bird Williams or a Bill McBride.

Ballad collecting can be high adventure. It has given me some of my most interesting friends, like Old Man Stobey of Miles City, Montana, the Swanson boys from the Washington woods, Charley Trollope of Waco, Nebraska, Bill Carlisle, the lone bandit from Laramie, Wyoming, Captain Maitland of Snug Harbor, New York, and "Doc" Leslie of Deadwood, South Dakota, as well as the many lumberjacks in the Great Lakes country. The life in the outdoors will be relived when I no longer can sleep in the open and laugh at a rain or a snow. Best of all, faith in America grows as one becomes acquainted with the "folks."

The one-time thriving village of Long Rapids, which was settled by Irish, has long been silent; but the last strains of their wit and humor still return among those who can remember the barber, the hotel-keeper, the butcher, the missionaries, and the grocers, and most of all the weary lumbermen who followed the downward drive of logs on their way down the North Branch River to Alpena.

Neil Nevins, who worked in lumber camps when he was thirteen, recalls this favorite among the boys around Long Rapids. It seems the camp barber thought he was a master craftsman and started a shop of his own to get rich with dime shaves and two-bit haircuts. This song was composed after he opened his shop and started business.

SWEET LOVE OF GOD SHAVE

1   In a wee little village not far from this spot
A barber he set up a neat little shop.
With washing and shaving and men at their ease,
They walk right in and they do what they please.

Chorus
With a ya-you-yad-a-lum, ya-you-yad-a-lum
Lather and shave my frizz-a-ly chin.

2   Then a very bad habit he said he must stop:
To never let trust come into his shop.
So he got an old razor all gaps and all rust
To shave the poor devil who came in on trust.

3   One day an Irishman was passing that way,
Whose beard had been growing for many a day.
So Paddy stepped in with a sigh and a nod,
"Do give me a shave for the sweet love of God."

4   "Well, come in," said the barber. "Sit down in the chair.
Your grizzly old beard won't amount to a hair."
The lather he spread over Paddy's big chin.
With the rusty old razor the job he begin.

5   "Oh, murder!" cried Pat. "I'm shaved with a tweezer,
     A love of God's shave with the devil's own razor."
     Old Paddy jumped up with a terrible roar
     And bolted right out at that open door.

6   Next day as Paddy was passing the door
     A jackass he let out a terrible roar.
     "Oh, murder!" cried Pat. "That vagabond knave
     Is giving some friend a sweet love of God shave."

THE WILD COLONIAL BOY

William Anning of Ann Arbor, who followed the woods from Maine to British Columbia, called attention to Robert Frost's mention of *Wild Colonial Boy* in *Witch of Coos:*
"Of his old song, *The Wild Colonial Boy,* He always used to sing along the tote-road."
At Turner's Camp on the Chippewa were sung three "bad man" songs from Australia: *The Wild Colonial Boy, Bold Jack Dono-*

1   There was a noted hero, Jack Dolan was his name;
     Brought up by honest parents, he was reared near
          Castlemain.
     He was his father's only pride and his mother's only
          joy,
     And dearly did his parents love their wild Colonial
          boy.

hue, and *Johnnie Troy.* They were sung in many camps in the northern lumber woods. It would be interesting to learn exactly how the Australian songs got into the lumber camps of the United States.

Simon Close of Birch Run and Mrs. William Garchow of Farwell supplied these verses.

2   It was at the early age of sixteen he left his happy home,
And to Australia's sunny lands was most inclined to roam.
He robbed the rich and helped the poor; he stopped George McElroy,
Who trembling gave up his gold to the wild Colonial boy.

3   Then he bade the squire "Good morning" and he told him to beware
To never send a poor boy up while acting on the square;
And never part a mother from her only pride and joy,
For fear he might go rambling like this wild Colonial boy.

4   It was at the age of eighteen years he began his wild career,
With a heart that knows no danger and a spirit that has no fear.
He robbed the rich esquires, and their flocks he did destroy;
He was a terror to Australia, this wild Colonial boy.

5 One day upon the prairie, as Jack he rode along,
Listening to the mockingbirds singing their sweetest
  song,
Up rose a mount of troopers: Kelly, Davis, Gilroy;
They all rode up to capture him, this wild Colonial boy.

6 "Surrender now, Jack Dolan, for you see there's three
  to one,
Surrender in the Queen's name, for you're a plundering
  son."
Jack drew two pistols from his side and held them up
  on high.
"I'll fight, but not surrender," cried this wild Colonial
  boy.

7 Then he fired a shot at Kelly that brought him to the
  ground,
And in return from Davis he received his fatal wound.
Then a pistol ball pierced the proud heart from the
  pistol of Gilroy,
And that's the way they captured the wild Colonial
  boy.

Of the three Australian songs sung in the Michigan camps, the most popular was *Bold Jack Donohue*.

Some would sing of Johnnie Troy
  And some of the "Cumberland" crew,
But of all the songs, that I liked best
  Was of bold Jack Donohue.

Bill McBride of Isabella City, Perry Allen of Shepherd, Tom Maloney of Limestone, and Mrs. Ed Rusch of Standish sang this one.

BOLD JACK DONOHUE

1 Come all you bold undaunted men,
  You outlaws of the day,
It's time to beware of the ball and chain
  And also slavery.

2 Attention pay to what I say,
  And verily if you do,
I will relate the actual fate
  Of bold Jack Donohue.

3 He scarcely had landed, as I tell you,
  Upon Australia's shore,
Than he became a real highwayman
  As he had been before.

4 There was Underwood and Mackerman,
  And Wade and Westley, too—
These were the four associates
  Of bold Jack Donohue.

5   Jack Donohue, who was so brave,
        Rode out that afternoon,
    Knowing not that the pain of death
        Would overtake him soon.

6   So quickly then the horse police
        From Sydney came in view.
    "Be gone from here, you cowardly dogs,"
        Says bold Jack Donohue.

7   The captain and the sergeant
        Stopped then to decide,
    "Do you intend to fight us,
        Or unto us resign?"

8   "To surrender to such cowardly dogs
        Is more than I will do.
    This day I'll fight if I lose my life,"
        Says bold Jack Donohue.

9   The captain and the sergeant
        The men they did divide.
    They fired from behind him
        And also from each side.

10   It's six police he did shoot down
            Before the fatal ball
      Did pierce the heart of Donohue
            And cause bold Jack to fall.

11   And when he fell he closed his eyes;
            He bade the world adieu.
      Come all you boys and sing the song
            Of bold Jack Donohue.

Though some of the jacks sing of Johnny Try, most of those who know this Australian song call him Johnny Troy; Try and Troy are not pronounced too differently in Australian English. All three of these Australian imports seem to be well known to lumberjacks of New England and the Great Lakes, and not unknown to those of the Northwest.

This version was recalled by Bill McBride, Perry Allen, and Tom Dunn.

JOHNNIE TROY

1   Come all you daring bushrangers and outlaws of the
            land
      Who mean to live in slavery and wear a convict
            band!—
      I'd rather be a highwayman than be a convict bound
      For seven long years in New South Wales our trials
            for to stand.

2   There were four and twenty convicts coming down in
        one launch,
Some of them for seven years and more for a lower
        branch.
Troy, he espied them and solemnly swore,
"This very night I'll set you free; your trials are no
        more."

3   There was Johnnie Troy, Bell Hetherington, Joe Jack-
        son, and John Dunn;
There were four as fine young men as ever handled
        gun.
Said Troy unto his comrades, "Load every man his
        piece,
For this very night I'm bound to fight those mounted
        horse police."

4   As Troy and his gang were mounted, and they were
        going away,
They met an old man; he was traveling on his way.
"Your watch and chain right instantly! And that I do
        demand,
Or this very night I'll blow out your brains if you re-
        fuse to stand."

5   "For a watch and chain, I've got none," the old man
        did say.
"For keeping of a large family I have to work each day.
I was banished from my native shore for being a brave
        wild boy."
"If that be so, you'll not be wronged," said daring John-
        nie Troy.

6   They scarcely sailed a league or two when they began
        to row.
But three well-armed policemen sat seated in the bow.
To their surprise, being in disguise, Troy on them did
        rush,
For he knew he had three comrades bold concealed in
        ambush.

7   "Now we have gained our launch, brave boys, we'll
        pull a brave stiff oar.
We'll smash and break those iron bands before we
        reach the shore.
We'll smash and break those iron bands, and we'll stone
        the horse police.
We'll them amaze and sing the praise of the convicts'
        quick release."

8   Now Troy he was arrested and was condemned to die,
To die upon the scaffold of Sydney gallows high.
The poor crowded round the scaffold, and dismal was
    their cry:
"There goes a bold, undaunted youth. His name was
    Johnnie Troy!"

THE FATE OF THE "CUMBERLAND" CREW

This "Cumberland" ballad of 1862 commemorated the destruction of the Union sloop by the spectacular iron-clad "Merrimac." The song was known to Bill Monigal of Iron Mountain, Silver Jack Swan of Gladstone, John Shanahan of Escanaba, Benjamin Needham of Flint, and Art Mulford of St. Louis, whose version this is.

1   Oh, shipmates, come gather and join in my ditty
    Of a terrible battle that happened of late.
Let each good Union tar shed a sad tear of pity
    When he thinks of the once gallant "Cumberland's" fate.

2   On the eighth day of March is told the sad story,
    And many a brave tar bade this world adieu;
But our flag was wrapped in a mantle of glory
    By the heroic deeds of the "Cumberland" crew.

3 On that ill-fated day, about ten in the morning,
  The sky was cloudless and bright shone the sun,
And the drums of the "Cumberland" sounded the
  warning
  That told every seaman to stand by his gun.

4 When an ironclad frigate down on us came bearing,
  And high in the air the rebel flag flew;
The pennant of rebellion she proudly was wearing,
  Determined to conquer the "Cumberland" crew.

5 Then up spoke our brave captain, with stern resolution,
  Saying, "Boys, this monster will not be dismayed.
We have sworn to protect our beloved Constitution;
  And die for our country we are not afraid.

6 "We will fight for our country; our cause it is glorious.
  To the stars and the stripes we will stand ever
  true.
We will sink at our quarters or conquer victorious!"
  He was answered with cheers from the "Cumber-
  land" crew.

7 Then our gallant ship fired. Her guns loudly thundered.
   Her broadside like hail on the rebels did pour.
But the sailors gazed on, struck with terror, and
   wondered
   When the shot struck her side silently o'er.

8 But the pride of our navy would never be daunted,
   Though the dead and the wounded our deck they
     did strew:
The star-spangled banner how proudly she flaunted,
   Sustained by the blood of the "Cumberland"
     crew.

9 They fought us nine hours with stern resolution,
   Till the rebels found cannon would never avail.
The flag of secession had no power to gall them,
   Though the blood of our boys was dyeing the
     blue.

10 She struck us amidships; our planks she did sever.
   Her sharp iron prong struck through our ship
     sore;
And as slowly they sank 'neath Virginia's waters,
   Their voices on earth never will be heard more.

11 In their battle-stained graves they are silently lying;
   Their voices to earth have long bade adieu;
 Yet the star-spangled banner above them is flying,
   'Twas nailed to the mast by the "Cumberland"
    crew.

12 Columbia's sweet birthright of freedom's communion,
   The flag, never floated so proudly before,
 For the spirits of those who have died for the Union
   Above its broad folds now exultingly soar.

13 And when our brave sailors in battle assemble,
   God bless our dear banner—the red, white, and
    blue.
 Beneath its bright stars we'll cause tyrants to tremble
   Or sink at our guns like the "Cumberland" crew.

INDEX

OF

SONGS

AND

POEMS

1244